*** the Monks of Mt. Tabor
M Monastery of the H.Transfiguration
17001 Tomki Rd-(707)485-8959
E. Redwood Valley, CA 95470

ON THE OTHER SIDE

by Marvin Ford
as told to Dave Balsiger
and Don Tanner

D0499578

LOGOS INTERNATIONAL
Plainfield, New Jersey

ON THE OTHER SIDE
Copyright © 1978 by Marvin Ford,
David Balsiger, Don Tanner
All rights reserved
Printed in the United States of America
Library of Congress Catalog Card Number: 78-52065
International Standard Book Number: 0-88270-310-2
Logos International, Plainfield, New Jersey 07061

Table of Contents

In Loving Dedication

To my dear wife, Olive Elizabeth, a faithful companion at my side these many years, a great source of inspiration and help, and a contributor to much of this book, and to those intercessors in prayer who daily undergird our ministry.

Marvin S. Ford

Preface

The use of occultic material in this book does not imply my endorsement of nonbiblical concepts or experiences.

Certain elements of out-of-the-body incidents are common among Christian and non-Christian accounts. Occultic theories and non-Christian stories are included to show the contrasts between spiritual reality and satanic counterfeit.

The names and address locations of some individuals mentioned in this book have been changed to protect their identity.

—Marvin Ford

Acknowledgments

Many long hours of research, writing and editing have gone into producing this book. I am grateful for the collaboration of Dave Balsiger and Don Tanner, whose professional assistance during my extensive travels and rigorous schedule of speaking engagements on the subject has made this manuscript possible. I also am grateful to Bruce and Martha Anderson for their valuable contributions in research, editing and typing, and to my wife, Olive, for her remarkable memory and meticulous care to ensure the accuracy of many details relating to my experience and our ministry together through the years.

Introduction

On The Other Side is a unique and intriguing presentation on the subject of afterlife. In the past few months I have traveled to most of the major cities of the United States, appearing on many leading radio and television stations and giving interviews to scores of newspapers. The openness in talking about death and the hereafter that I have observed has been both exciting and revealing. Much is being learned on this tremendous topic that will help people in a practical way.

Having known Marvin Ford and his family for more than twenty-five years, I consider him to be very sound emotionally and a man of great integrity. It was a joy to share Marvin's moment of triumph when he returned from the beyond, and it has been even more thrilling to observe the changes in his life and the successes of his ministry as they became known worldwide.

Reading this thrilling book, you will live in a new realm of anticipation—awaiting a greater life *on the other side*.

Dr. Ralph Wilkerson
Author of *Beyond and Back*
Minister of Melodyland

1

Journeys into the Light

Surely most of us have wondered how it would feel to pop out of our bodies and travel through space at the speed of thought, perhaps to some distant planet.

It happens every day.

I have experienced it; so can you.

Like a cork exploding from a bottle, my spirit once pulled free from my body and ascended at a 45-degree angle through the ceiling of the hospital room I lay in. I felt this essential "me" traveling at an incredible speed toward a brilliant light deep in outer space.

As I drew closer, the radiance of that light was brilliantly incandescent. In what seemed only seconds, I was looking down on the most magnificent city I had ever set eyes upon, dazzling with a million sparkling lights.

Though this celestial city is exactly as described in Revelation 21 of the Bible, no mortal words can adequately describe its glories; no artist can capture its splendor nor composer recreate its joyous melodies.

This magnificent metropolis is laid out symmetrically. I saw row upon row of brilliant colors. As I floated high above, I could see great distances to the massive gates of the city, each one a gigantic pearl, set in jasper walls—a sort of green with a vein running throughout like marble. The iridescence beckoned to me.

I fixed my gaze upon streets of gold, rising level upon level, and smooth as glass. I could see through those streets to observe my body lying on its hospital bed. The hospital appeared as though it had no roof, and I recognized people as they moved around the halls.

In the world beyond, distance means nothing; time means nothing. . . .

What I am about to reveal in these pages may startle you, for I have been on the other side, I have talked with Jesus Christ, and I have returned to this life with a mission of immense significance.

This is the story of my lifelong dream and how it was at last fulfilled on one New Year's Day when I died, went into the world beyond, and returned to a new and splendid life.

Many are wondering is it really possible to die, leave my body, journey to the other side and come back? Or are such experiences hallucinations? If there is a beyond, what is it like? Can I know where I am going after death?

And how could I be sure in my out-of-the-body experience that what I saw was real? What are the characteristics of on-the-other-side experiences; how can we detect self-deception?

Who is the "being of light" who appears and communicates with those who visit the other side?

What is the difference between Christian and non-Christian out-of-the-body phenomena, and can Christians experience astral projection?

Can we believe the reports of those who have seen the world beyond?

Such fascinating questions are answered here. As you turn these pages, you will travel to the beyond and feel the exhilaration of life at its fullest. You will also sense the dangers that lurk for those who enter the other side unprepared.

Ancients Who Saw the Light

More and more people in modern times are catching glimpses of the other side. For some it has been momentary. Others have for minutes or even hours beheld vistas of beautiful flowers of every color and tone, smelled aromas of surpassing fragrance, tasted delicious celestial fruit, touched massive, gem-studded pillars and colonnades of heavenly mansions, or listened in rapture to angelic choirs and orchestras.

While we cannot accept modern visions as rivals in authority to the Bible, precedence for such experiences is found in the Bible.

The Apostle Paul wrote in 2 Corinthians 12:2-4:

> I knew a man in Christ about fourteen years ago, (whether in the body, I cannot tell; or whether out of the body, I cannot tell: God knoweth;) . . . How that he was caught up into paradise, and heard unspeakable words. . . .

John, author of the biblical Book of Revelation, spent some time viewing the other side. He writes:

> And I John saw the holy city, new
> Jerusalem, coming down from God out of
> heaven, prepared as a bride adorned for
> her husband.[1]

He observed the city in detail and saw its twelve
foundations, massive jasper walls and gates of pearl,
its golden streets, fruit trees and crystal clear river.
He was given its measurements, discovered its
source of light and saw who lived there. He talked
with Jesus and beheld the city's past, present and
future telescoped in time.

The martyr Stephen is another who caught a
glimpse of this glory. He saw Jesus standing on the
right hand of God just moments before he was stoned
to death.[2]

The prophet Ezekiel witnessed crowning
glories,[3] and Daniel gazed upon the "Ancient of days
. . . whose garment was white as snow, and the hair
of his head like the pure wool: his throne was like the
fiery flame . . . a fiery stream issued and came forth
from before him: thousand thousands ministered
unto him, and ten thousand times ten thousand stood
before him. . . ."[4]

Moderns Who Have Seen the Light

A contemporary who has visited the other side is
Lorne Fox, missionary and world traveler. Escorted
by an angel, he was awed by the "symphony of
harmonic color," thrilled by the great numbers of
angels clad in white, shining garments, and stricken
with wonder at other heavenly beings clothed in
garments of amber.

Here is part of what he reported:

> I observed towers, minarets and domes

4

crowning magnificent structures. They towered high above greenswards. These, the angel told me, were the mansions which the Master had promised that He had gone to prepare.

. . . We walked along the winding roadway into a magnificent garden. I have seen the flowers of the far north, and the exquisite flowers of the far south, but nothing can compare with the color of flowers that bloom in that Eternal Land!

I was walking now, in the paradise garden within the heart of the kingdom of heaven! And it was there that I met many friends and loved ones, whom I recognized. My own little mother came to me, with her hands extended in welcome. She was perfect . . . young . . . radiant, as are all within those portals.[5]

Kenneth Hagin of Tulsa, Oklahoma, visited the other side. He gives this account:

We came to the throne of God, and I beheld it in all its splendor. I was not able to look upon the face of God, but only beheld His form.

I was first attracted to the rainbow about the throne. . . . Then to the winged creatures on either side. . . . They were peculiar looking creatures, and as I walked up with Jesus, these creatures stood with wings outstretched. They had eyes of fire set all the way around their heads, and they looked in all directions at once.

I stood with Jesus in the midst, about

eighteen to twenty-four feet from the throne. . . . I started to look at the One who sat upon the throne. Jesus told me not to look upon His face. I could see only a form. . . .

Then for the first time I actually looked into the eyes of Jesus . . . they looked like wells of living love . . . their tender look is indescribable. As I looked into His eyes, I fell at His feet.

His feet were bare, and I laid the palms of my hands on His feet and laid my forehead on the backs of my hands . . . I saw in the palms of His hands the wounds of the crucifixion—three-cornered, jagged holes. . . . I could see light on the other side of the hole.[6]

(Centuries ago, Christ's disciple Thomas put his finger into the same nailprints after Jesus was raised from the dead.)[7]

Marietta Davis, a young woman who lived during the mid-1800s in Berlin, New York, made one of the longest visits to the other side on record. Many witnesses, including her physician, Dr. Emerson Hull, attested to the genuineness of her experience. What she saw and heard during the nine days her body lay in a coma harmonizes with biblical teachings about the beyond. She, too, tells of being escorted by an angel and on one occasion saw a great city, which she describes in these excerpts:

Soon we emerged from the ascending gallery of rainbows and stood upon an aerial plain, resting in the transparent air above that magnificent and lofty dome

6

which crowns the center temple of instruction in the paradisical abode.

From this position I beheld the great city, reaching on every side beneath my view. Majestic trees in groups, and at regular intervals arose, bearing a profusion of fragrant and shining clusters of flowers. Beneath their shade . . . appeared minute flower beds, filled with every variety of flowers and blossoming shrubs and vines.

Fountains of living waters also were visible, some just rising from the green grass, and flowing through their marble channels, or through beds of golden sands, with a low and pleasant murmur; while others gushed forth in full volume to a lofty height, and descended in glowing streams. . . .

The city was divided into one hundred and forty-four great wards or divisions, arranged in a series of advancing degrees of sublimity and beauty. . . . Thus the entire city appeared one garden of flowers; one grove of umbrage; one gallery of sculptured imagery; one undulating sea of fountains; one unbroken extent of sumptuous architecture all set in a surrounding landscape of corresponding beauty, and overarched by a sky adorned with hues of immortal light that bathed and encircled each and every object. . . .[8]

In recent months many others have come forth with spine-tingling stories about their travels and encounters in the afterworld. Intriguing similarities emerge from their accounts.

2

Our Astonishing Talents

"After all my funeral expenses have been paid . . . sell all my property which is all in cash and stocks . . . and have this balance [of] money go into a research of some scientific proof [that the] soul of the human body leaves at death.

"I think in time there can be a photograph of the soul leaving the human at death." So wrote James Kidd, a seventy-year-old prospector in Phoenix, Arizona, who disappeared in 1949 on an expedition to the Superstition Mountains of Arizona, never to return. He was declared dead a few years later.

Kidd's challenge poses intriguing questions, the answers to which many of us seldom contemplate. In our modern, enlightened society, the existence of a person's soul or spiritual side is taken for granted by most. Even primitive tribes cling tenaciously to a belief in spirits and to some form of existence after death. But we all would like to make sure that man is more than his physical body.

What part of us can gaze upon a shimmering waterfall and marvel at its beauty? How do we explain our deep yearning within to reach into realms we can't see or touch? When we ascend the heights of joy or slide to the depths of bewilderment or despair, what is it inside that leaps with ecstasy or brings the sting of hot tears?

And we are all aware of those strange abilities we sometimes possess. It is difficult to explain intuition, ESP or *déjà vu* [1]—the feeling we've "been there" or "seen it" before, but know we haven't.

The Search Is On

The handwritten will of the bachelor James Kidd was found in 1964 in a Douglas, Arizona, bank safety deposit box, opened because the rent on it was long overdue. And after a lengthy Arizona court battle, the American Society for Psychical Research (ASPR), which was among 130 contenders, was granted Kidd's entire estate of $270,000 to undertake a scientific research for proof that the soul does exist.

Dr. Karlis Osis, research director for ASPR, believes it can be demonstrated that "some part of the human personality is capable of operating outside the body before and after death." [2]

The society's first objective was to study the observations of American doctors and nurses in 1,644 deathbed cases. "Most of the dying claimed to be able to see and talk with apparitions that had come to take them away to another existence—friends or relatives already dead," Dr. Osis says.

To check cultural differences, ASPR took a similar survey in India where, too, "patients reported that apparitions of dead people had come to take them away to another existence. But there was a difference," Dr. Osis notes. "Americans, with few exceptions, felt they were being taken away peacefully to a beautiful reunion with their dead relatives. But in India, one out of three patients saw themselves being taken away violently or against their will."

The society next asked newspaper readers to send in detailed accounts of personal out-of-the-body experiences, and more and more stories have come to light to help researchers detect patterns and similarities.

Out-of-the-body experiences are common among both the dying and the living. Such a discovery, after years of investigation into the phenomena, has convinced Dr. Osis "that people can actually leave their physical bodies and travel in different levels of reality and consciousness."[3]

He hopes ASPR will one day be able to capture a soul on film as it leaves the body, a proof of its existence. He says, "Specialists in physics and biology will help, using a wide array of supersensitive cameras and various other physical measuring devices." But he admits, "Proving the existence of a soul after death with hard, scientific evidence will be an extremely difficult job."[4]

Ingenious methods have been used by others in attempts to detect the escaping soul. One researcher, Duncan MacDouball, for example, believes the soul has weight. In his experiments he weighed dying patients on a scale, hoping to time the flight of their souls upon death. As they died, he detected a slow, but gradual loss of body weight. This he attributed to a physiological loss of moisture through breathing and perspiration. One subject he observed lost twenty-eight grams per hour. At death, however, the patient suddenly lost twenty-one grams, possibly indicating the departure of the soul.[5]

An unusual photographic process has detected a halo-like image surrounding the human body not unlike the auras around saints depicted in religious art. In the process known as Kirlian photography, an individual is placed directly on film and subjected to a high frequency electrical field. Photos are reproduced in total darkness without the aid of a camera or a light source other than the subject, who takes his own picture by the light he himself gives off.

This aura has been known to outline a missing finger as though it were still there. Two investigators of extrasensory perception (ESP) bring additional insight into this phenomenon. "Clairvoyants are quick to point out . . . that the aura is actually a misnomer; they believe the human body is interpenetrated by another body of energy, and it is the luminescence from this second body radiating outward that they see as the aura. We look, they say, something like an eclipse of the sun by the moon, the luminous astral body being completely concealed by the physical body. Paracelsus (1493-1541), the Swiss philosopher, chemist, alchemist and doctor, also believed that a half-corporeal, or 'star' body, lives in the flesh and is its mirror image."[6]

Does this body of energy have weight? Kirlian experiments have shown that a person's halo begins to fade as he approaches death, then slowly fades away to nothing after death. Other research has uncovered evidence of cloud-like substances that break away from the physical body at death. Could this be the phenomenon detected by the weight loss experiment?

Two Sides of Man

Much misunderstanding exists about the spiritual nature of man—that entity which we distinguish apart from the human body. While science has not developed an X-ray capable of detecting our nonphysical being, we do have ample evidence of its existence.

Our sensitivity to life's beauty, unrelated to our physical existence, is one proof. The experiences of thousands who have departed their bodies for journeys to the other side are testimony, too.

To silence the rationalizations of those who deny the realities of other-side phenomena, I assert that the most authoritative document for insight into spiritual dimensions is God's Word, the Bible. Its mysteries, miracles, stories and promises, its facts, principles and predictions, warnings, judgments and rewards—all these concern human life on both a physical and spiritual level. The Bible teaches the spiritual is two-dimensional and multifaceted.

And a Third Side

The Bible says man is spirit, soul and body.

> . . . The very God of peace sanctify you wholly; and I pray God your whole *spirit* and *soul* and *body* be preserved. . . .[7]
> . . . The word of God is quick, and powerful, and sharper than any two-edged sword, piercing even to the dividing asunder of soul and spirit, and of the joints and marrow [body]. . . .[8]

The body is external, fleshly and material. It is the house in which the soul and spirit dwell. At death, the inner being, composed of soul and spirit, leaves the body to continue in a state of full consciousness and life in the afterworld. The earthly body eventually disintegrates into dust—what it was made of originally.[9]

The soul is your I.D. It's your personality, the part you project to others. It's your contact with the world, your five senses.

With your soul, you see the rainbow arching through the clouds, smell the sweet fragrance of a gardenia, hear the laughter of a happy child, feel the tender touch of a lover and taste the delicious flavor of a fine peach. The body in which the soul dwells is but the physical sensor that permits contact. With your soul, you laugh or cry, love or hate, enjoy pleasure or dread pain, show indifference or feel passion.

The spirit is the real "you." It's the entity that lies dormant within an individual until it is quickened by the Holy Spirit when the individual is spiritually reborn. Some Bible scholars equate spirit with the mind; others declare that the spirit is synonymous with the soul.

From my study of the Bible, I see the mind as a bridge between the soul and spirit. It is this bridge that knows, decides and wills. The mind can compute complicated formulae and decipher abstract concepts, solve perplexing problems and determine destinies, store knowledge and impart truth. More importantly, the mind or will determines the extent to which the spirit rules the soul or vice versa. Although the body and soul are involved, it is the spirit entity of our inner being that worships God and communicates with those beyond.

The spirit and soul are separate and distinct parts of the inner person, just as together they are distinct from the body. Man is a spirit who has a soul and lives in a body. While unique in their parts, the spirit

13

and soul are a unity, and at physical death this inner being continues to live. Death, as we know it, is but the separation of the spiritual and physical.[10]

If the body is the physical sensor of the soul and the house of the spirit, how do we touch the invisible world, and how do we see ourselves outside the body?

Our Invisible Double

Most people who have an out-of-the-body experience are so preoccupied with events and scenes around them that they don't observe their spiritual body. Such was my experience. Many who have visited the other side, though, claim they did see their own form or the entities of departed friends and relatives.

Those who describe the spirit say it resembles the physical body in several ways, and that it has powers unlimited by time, space or matter. Their descriptions are too similar to discount them as hallucinatory.

Before we examine the spiritual body, let's see what the Bible says about it. Apostle Paul wrote:

> But some man will say, How are the dead raised up? and with what body do they come? Thou fool . . . [of] that which thou sowest, thou sowest not that body that shall be, but bare grain. . . . But God giveth it a body as it hath pleased him, and to every seed his own body. . . . There are also celestial bodies, and bodies terrestrial: but the glory of the celestial is one, and the glory of the terrestrial is another. . . . So also is the resurrection of the dead. It is sown in corruption; it is raised in

14

> incorruption: It is sown in dishonour; it is
> raised in glory: it is sown in weakness; it is
> raised in power: It is sown a natural body; it
> is raised a spiritual body. There is a natural
> body, and there is a spiritual body.
>
> (1 Corinthians 15:35-44)

Paul's reference to the spiritual body corresponds with the accounts of many who have had out-of-the-body experiences. The inadequacy of human vocabulary to describe the afterworld body has been a major obstacle for people who have seen their spirits. While they often agree on the properties and general characteristics of the spirit, they use varying analogies—a filmy piece of gray chiffon, an amorphous cloud, "something resembling human form"—in their efforts to describe what they saw.

If we acknowledge that things exist in the spiritual dimension with which there is nothing to compare in the material, and that a mere mortal's sketches of afterworld grandeur are inadequate, how much more spectacular and magnificent must be the realities of the world beyond!

Because an account may seem unbelievable, we need not automatically discredit it.

In judging such experiences, we must be wary of possible deceptions. Some realms of the beyond are illusory.

A fine line exists between the realities and the illusions of the other side. Here are some questions to test the difference:

First, *is what the person describes corroborated by the Bible?*

Second, most people see far more than is recorded in the Bible. This doesn't invalidate their experience because God's Word provides only a glimpse into the beyond. The question to ask is, *does their account harmonize with biblical truth?*

Third, *how does the person see Christ?* Is He a being of kindly light who reaffirms the individual's goodness? Or is He the Savior whose blood was shed on Calvary for the remission of sin?

Fourth, *is there any change in the individual after he returns to his body?* Is his life different, or is he left bewildered, or with a false sense of security about his eternal destiny?

Fifth, *is the individual led to glorify God and uplift the name of Jesus?*

Sixth, if the person does not claim to know God, *is a need for God awakened or strengthened in him?*

We can accept an account if it is corroborated by or is consistent with Bible teachings, if the individual involved has a positive faith in Jesus Christ, and if there is no false concept of the destiny of those who go into the beyond unprepared by a personal relationship with Christ. At the same time, we must recognize human limitations in relating out-of-the-body experiences.

What Some Have Seen

Here are some accounts by those who have described the appearance of the human spirit. Christian and occult, they show similarities, but differ in significant aspects, depending on the destiny of the spirit.

Dr. Raymond A. Moody, Jr., whose book *Life After Life* has sparked wide interest in what lies beyond, made startling discoveries during his five-year study of afterworld phenomena. He interviewed fifty people who had departed their bodies for brief periods, observing that they first

became aware of their spirit doubles either by what they were not able to do or by amazing abilities.
   He writes:

> They find, when out of their physical bodies, that although they may try desperately to tell others of their plight, no one seems to hear them.
>
> To complicate the fact that he is apparently inaudible to people around him, the person in a spiritual body soon finds that he is also invisible to others. . . . His spiritual body also lacks solidity; physical objects in the environment appear to move through it with ease, and he is unable to get a grip on any object or person he tries to touch.
>
> Further, it is invariably reported that this spiritual body is also weightless. Most first notice this when they find themselves floating right up to the ceiling of the room, or into the air . . . in fact, quite a few persons have commented to me that they were aware of the lack of the physical sensations of body weight, movement, and position sense while in their spiritual bodies.
>
> Finally, almost everyone remarks upon the timelessness of this out-of-body state. [11]

The spiritual body may be limited in the sense that it can't grasp a knob to open a door, but it can just go through the door. With physical objects no barrier, Moody observes, travel is unhindered and can be at the speed of thought.
   Several of those he interviewed described their

spirits variously as having density, though cloudlike or wispy; as transparent energy, yet with parts such as arms and legs; as roundish in form, but with a definite top and bottom; or as possessing the senses of sight and hearing, yet unable to touch the space-time world.

According to the *Tibetan Book of the Dead*, when a person departs from his physical form, he notices he is still in a body. It is portrayed as a "shining" body, which has no material substance. Moody observes:

> Thus, he can go through rocks, walls, and even mountains without encountering any resistance. Travel is almost instantaneous. Wherever he wishes to be, he arrives there in only a moment. His thought and perception are less limited; his mind becomes very lucid, and his senses seem more keen and more perfect and closer in nature to the divine. If he has been in physical life blind or deaf or crippled, he is surprised to find that in his "shining" body all his senses, as well as all the powers of his physical body, have been restored and intensified.
>
> In short . . . it is quite obvious that there is a striking similarity between the account in this manuscript and the events which have been related to me by twentieth-century Americans.[12]

Robert A. Monroe, a Virginia businessman and founder of Mind Research Institute who began experimenting many years ago with astral projection, an occult practice in which the spirit double leaves the body and travels in a spiritual realm, gives a detailed description of his spirit. His portrayal not only corroborates the testimony of others who say the double has human semblance, it adds intriguing new insights.

On numerous occasions, through various techniques, he was able to lift out of his physical body and either remain in the room, travel to various parts of the United States, or go deeper into the unknown regions of the beyond. In the late 1950s and early '60s he observed his out-of-the-body form. Here are some excerpts from his account:

I was again on the couch, feeling very smooth vibrations. I opened my eyes and looked around, and everything seemed normal. . . . I then moved my arms, which were folded, and stretched them upward as I lay on my back. They felt outstretched, and I was surprised when I looked, for there were my arms still folded over my chest.

I looked upward to where I felt them, and I saw the shimmering outlines of my arms and hands in exactly the place they felt they were! I looked back at the folded arms, then at the bright shadow of them outstretched. I could see through them to the bookshelves beyond. It was like a bright, glowing outline which moved when I felt them move or made them move willfully. I wiggled my fingers, and the glowing fingers wiggled, and I felt them wiggle. I put my hands together, and I felt my hands clasp each other. They felt just like ordinary hands, no different.

Visually, I could see my arms folded over

my chest. Simultaneously, I could see the glowing outline of my hands and arms reaching out above me. I tried to move the physical arms, but could not do so. I tried to move the glowing arm-outlines, and they "worked" perfectly.

I tried to feel with my physical arms, but could determine no sensation. With the glowing outline arms, I clasped my hands together, and they felt completely normal. I rubbed the outline hands over each outline forearm, and the arms felt normal, solid to the touch. I moved one outline hand to the shelf by the cot, and I couldn't feel the shelf! My outline hand went right through it.[13]

Monroe calls this "glowing outline" the second body, which he concludes is similar to that of the physical. When his spirit hands touched each other, they felt solid. But when he touched the shelf, nothing. The spirit world would seem to be just as tangible to the second body as is the material world to the physical body. The spirit can be seen, felt, heard, and touched on the other side just as the physical body is in this world. But there can be no crossing over except visually. Those beyond can see this side. Except for an act of the supernatural, however, we cannot peer into the other side.

Many ask, "If the spirit has substance, how can it inhabit a physical body?" A material object is composed of perhaps billions of atoms continually whirling in their orbits. Scientists say the human body contains about one octillion atoms. On a minute scale, spaces exist between the atom comparable to the distances between the stars in their orbits.

Within these spaces, the human spirit can occupy a physical body and retain its form. Of what substance this form is, no one knows. But the spirit's composition is obviously of another plane. When it departs the body, it is free to travel in the dimension to which it is naturally tuned.

This also explains how demon entities can enter and inhabit a human being unprotected by a personal relationship with Christ. In such cases, the body houses not only the human double, but one or many other spirit entities. Such a possibility warns of the dangers inherent in occult entanglement. Evil spirits roam the other side searching for willing hosts through which they can enjoy the benefits of both dimensions.

Monroe made another fascinating discovery about his second body. He continues:

> I was out of the physical . . . staying in the same room. Again I noticed the strange rubbery elasticity of this other body. I could stand in the middle of the room and reach out to touch the wall some eight feet away.
>
> At first, my arm didn't come anywhere near the wall. Then I kept pushing my hand outward, and suddenly the texture of the wall was against my hand. Just by pushing out, my arm had stretched to twice its length without my noticing anything different. When I relaxed the pushing out, the arm came back and seemed normal.
>
> This confirms the other evidence that you can make it just about whatever shape you think of, consciously or unconsciously.

If left alone, it reverts to your normal humanoid shape.[14]

Is the spirit elastic? Can it really take different forms at the whim of the individual? Perhaps. But let us beware of what we hear or read about the spirit world. Much deception exists. Monroe's experience may be valid, but whenever one dabbles in the occult, he is vulnerable to powers of deception.

Monroe does corroborate the testimony of Christians who have described the appearance of the second body in the afterlife. The departed in Heaven are seen living with real and visible spiritual bodies, clothed in garments of light. "Their appearance is in such glorious splendor that no language can describe them," one witness reports.

Among those who have visited the other side is Seneca Sodi, a Christian Greek-Jew from Scandinavia. In the early 1900s, he detailed many scenes of a city of splendor in the afterworld to a Quaker minister.

Sodi said:

> As I . . . began to mingle more freely with the group of joyous spirits, I met some whom I recognized as old friends. I cannot tell how we recognized each other, but there is such a similarity of the spirit itself to the bodily features that we at once knew each other, and memory was so fresh that we seemed never to have forgotten anyone.[15]

General William Booth, founder of the Salvation Army, was another who not only saw the other side, but saw the patriarchs and apostles of ancient times and myriads of spirits who once lived on Earth.[16]

According to his account and the stories of many other credible witnesses, the form or outline of the second body always is humanoid.

This poses another intriguing question. What gender does the spirit resemble? Man? Woman? General Booth gives some insight here in his account of meeting two persons in the heavenly city. Of one, Booth said:

> He was at the same time earthly and celestial . . . from instinct, I felt that the being before me was a man, a redeemed and glorified man. He looked at me, and I could not help but return his gaze.

After some narrative, Booth describes the other person he encountered:

> My former visitor, I have said, was a glorious man; this was the glorified form of a woman. She told me her name. I had heard it on earth. . . .[17]

While the Bible teaches that male-female relationships do not exist in Heaven, [18] it is not unbelievable that the spirit—in its resemblance of physical form—can appear as it really was on Earth. All, of course, are equal before Christ, for in Him we are neither male nor female.[19] Could, then, the appearances of male and female form be for the recognition of loved ones?[20]

Another interesting aspect of the spirit's appearance is light. "Persons" in Heaven are reported as surrounded by an aura of rainbow hues so brilliant, witnesses say, that mortal eye cannot gaze upon it. The aura, which may vary with the individual according to spiritual attainment, gives one the appearance of being clothed in white. Yet this light contains all the prismatic colors of the rainbow in infinite variety.

While on the other side, I saw light beings—literally millions of them—moving in perfect harmony. No one had light of his own; each was a reflection of the glory of God.

Marietta Davis adds another dimension to the spirit's appearance in her description of friends she met in the beyond:

> Although I knew them, their appearance was unlike that while upon earth . . . they appeared all mind, all light, all glory, all adoration, all love supremely pure, all peace and calm serenity, all united in sublime employ, all expression of heavenly unfolding joy.[21]

Marietta's perception focuses on the spiritual qualities of the departed in Heaven, whose robes are described by author Rebecca Springer in *Intra Muros:*

> Beneath the trees, in many happy groups, were little children, laughing and playing, running hither and thither in their joy. All through the grounds older people were walking, sometimes in groups, sometimes alone, but all with an air of peacefulness and happiness that made itself felt by me, even a stranger.
>
> All were in spotless white, though many wore about them or carried in their hands clusters of beautiful flowers. As I looked

upon their happy faces and their spotless robes, again I thought, "These are they . . . which have washed their robes, and made them white in the blood of the Lamb."

The material out of which my robe was fashioned was unlike anything that I had ever seen. It was soft and light and shone with a faint luster, reminding me more of silk crepe than anything I could recall, only infinitely more beautiful. It fell about me in soft graceful folds. . . .[22]

Her account is corroborated in Revelation 3:5, "He that overcometh, the same shall be clothed in white raiment. . . ."

These accounts demonstrate that the spirit and soul exist after physical death as an entity resembling the human body. The spiritual double—the real you—has substance tangible in the beyond. It can wear clothes, be handled, see, hear, talk, and is even more conscious than when in the physical.

The Bible supports this. If the human spirit has no substance or form, if it is but energy or an intellectual entity, how could Moses—out of his body—wear clothes and talk with Christ on the so-called Mount of Transfiguration? How could he have been seen with natural eyes if he wasn't real?[23] How could the rich man in Hades have a tongue and other bodily parts in his spiritual state if his inner being didn't have these parts?[24] How could the souls of the departed be seen clothed in white garments while out of their physical bodies unless there was a real spiritual body to wear the clothes?[25] And how could Christ's spirit go to Paradise and preach while His earthly body was in the grave if His inner self was immaterial and unreal?[26]

Destiny's Children

Another fascinating fact emerges from the ASPR study. The appearance of the double, though humanoid, is affected by its destiny. In Heaven, spirits are clothed in white garments and surrounded by varying degrees of light and color. In the abode of the lost, the second body takes on the semblance of the nether world.

One of the most vivid portrayals of this again comes from Marietta Davis, who was taken on a brief journey below. She writes:

> I fell as one precipitated from some dizzy height. The embodiment of darkness opened to receive me . . . and as I descended, the ever-accumulating weight of darkness pressed more fearfully upon me.
>
> At length a nether plane that seemed boundless was imaged upon my sight, which, at a little distance, appeared to be covered with the sparkling semblance of vegetation. . . .
>
> Multitudes of spirits appeared. . . . Some wore crowns upon their heads; others tiaras; and others decorations of which I knew not the name. Others wore towering helmets; and others circlets filled with glistening and waving plumes. . . .
>
> Kings and queens appeared arrayed in the gorgeous robes of coronation. Groups of nobility of both sexes also were decorated with all the varieties of adornment displayed in the pageantry of kingly courts.

Dense multitudes were visible in costume proper to the highly cultivated nations; and as they passed by, I discovered similar groups composed of less civilized tribes, attired in barbaric ornaments of every form.

While some appeared clothed in the habiliments of the present day, others were in ancient attire; but every class of spirits manifested, in the midst of variety of mode, a uniformity of external pride, pomp, and rapidly moving and dazzling luster.[27]

On the surface this description seems attractive. And it parallels the appearances of departed mothers, fathers, children, and friends, seen by many who have visited realms of the other dimension. But the nether world, though as real as Heaven, is a realm where illusion creates its own torment.

Such was Marietta's discovery as a spirit approached her whom she had known on Earth. She continues:

This being appeared externally far more brilliant than when in the body. The form, the countenance, the eyes, the hands, appeared endued with a metallic luster that varied with every motion and every thought.

Accosting me the spirit said . . . "My life on earth was suddenly brought to a close; and as I departed from the world, I moved rapidly in the direction prompted by my ruling desires. I rushed in haste to the enjoyment of the glittering scenes which you now behold.

"I was welcomed with gay and sportive sounds. I found myself endued with the power of strange and restless motion. I became conscious of a strange pervasion of the brain, and the cerebral organs became subject to a foreign power, which seemed to operate by an absolute possession.

"I inwardly crave to satisfy my hunger and my thirst, and the desire appears to create without and around me a tantalizing illusion of cool waters I may never drink, and grateful fruits I may never taste, and refreshing airs I never feel, and peaceful slumbers I may never enjoy.

"I know the forms around me are fantastic and delusive, yet every object appears to hold controlling power, and to domineer with cruel enchantment over my bewildered mind.

"This realm, curtained with a cloud of nether night, is one sea of perverted and diseased magnetic element. Here lust, pride, hate, avarice, love of self, ambition, contention, and blasphemies, reveling in madness, kindle into a burning flame. And that specialty of evil which does not belong to and unfold from one spirit, belongs to and unfolds from another; so that the combined strength of the aggregate of all is the prevailing law. By this strength of evil I am bound, and in it I exist. . . ."

Here she paused and fixed her eyes, wild with despair, upon me. I shrank from the dreadful glare, for the appearance manifested inexpressible torture.[28]

Mystical Mysteries

In this chapter we have followed the penetrating probes to prove that a soul exists. We have viewed with amazement the astonishing portraits of the human double painted with eyewitness artistry. And we have noted how destiny affects the appearance of the second body. Many fascinating questions about the afterlife remain.

3

Explorations into the Unknown

Mary Lois Leath of Texas looked down at her torn body and saw her seven-year-old son frantically tugging at her lifeless arm.

"Please! Somebody help mommy! Help mommy!" he wailed.

Wanting to console him, she felt helpless out of her body, hovering high above her mangled car.

"A crowd gathered as the ambulance and police cars arrived," she relates. "I watched as the police worked to free my body from the wreckage. I couldn't feel a thing as they lifted my body and put it into the ambulance with my son. Then I followed the ambulance carrying my body to the hospital."

Floating invisibly in the emergency room, Mrs. Leath watched as doctors feverishly worked to bring her back to life, sensing a pull from her lifeless body like the tug of a magnet as they began to succeed. Suddenly, she felt agonizing pain and the sensation of needles being injected into the flesh. Mary Leath had returned.[1]

Thelma Fritsche of Oregon suffered a near fatal heart attack in 1963 while hospitalized in a California medical center. Just after eight P.M. on March 30, a giant force seemed to be crushing her chest.

"Suddenly, I was hovering near the ceiling of my room, looking down at my body on the bed. As I floated there over the bed, I watched the doctors and nurses working feverishly over my worthless body, and I wondered why they didn't just leave it alone," she says.

Mrs. Fritsche observed them lift an arm and drop it, then lift a leg and drop it. She heard a nurse yell, "Hurry up! Hurry up!" and watched as they forced oxygen into her lungs. Reentering her body, Mrs. Fritsche felt sick and cheated, no longer free from suffering.[2]

Alice Parker of Kentucky longs to return to the sweet-smelling place where she felt soft breezes and where lovely music filled her ears. She "died" in 1944 of complications following a gall bladder operation.

"Suddenly, I started floating away as my spirit left my body," she recalls. "I looked down on my heartbroken family. I could hear my father pleading through his sobs, 'Please don't leave us.' But I drifted farther away.

"As I floated higher, I could smell the sweet scent of roses and lilacs. It was beautiful. I could hear the soft music of harps."

Apparently it was not her time to go either, for she soon felt dreadful pain and awakened in her body.[3]

Elizabeth Wilkes of Miami was driving down the street when a milk truck smashed into her car. Her next awareness was a floating sensation as she slipped away from her body, hurled to the pavement by the impact.

"I saw a beautiful white and gold light," she reports. "It was like a beam of sunlight coming through a cloud, only a thousand times more beautiful.

"I began moving toward the light. It was an incredible feeling. I wasn't aware of physical things . . . I felt strangely happy and at home. I wanted to float toward the light, but turned to look back at my body.

"There it was, eyes closed and unconscious, lying on the stretcher in the ambulance. One attendant was giving me oxygen and also working on the wounds on my face. The other was trying feverishly to block the flow of blood coming from my leg.

"The next thing I remember I began to spin in space and then I was in a hospital with my face completely covered with bandages except for my eyes and mouth. . . ."[4]

The Skeptic Doubts

Skeptics want more than such testimonies to convince them that there is an "other side." These recollections neither prove nor disprove anything, they argue, for so-called out-of-the-body episodes can be nothing more than physiological and neurological reactions caused by near death-induced biological trauma.

But if people are hallucinating, how do we explain the remarkable similarities in their reports?

If one has not experienced death, nor listened to others tell about the afterlife, it is easy to call these accounts mere imaginings. But the sincerity, warmth, and feeling with which all, without exception, recall the other side cannot be captured in a printed story.

Those of us who have experienced the other side are not victims of psychoses. We're ordinary people who hold jobs and in some cases positions of importance; we carry out our assignments responsibly. We enjoy normal relationships with families and friends. We know the difference between a dream and being awake. And whether we were dead or near death, our out-of-the-body travels were as real as eating a ham sandwich.

Common Story Elements

Out-of-the-body travel happens every time a person dies and quite often when one suffers severe physical trauma. Before the development of modern resuscitation techniques, few returned to tell about it.

While no two experiences are alike in all their details, and coincidence is blind and patternless, researchers today see many common elements in such reports. And it is highly unlikely that a mother in Texas, a heart attack victim in Oregon, a Kentucky surgery case, or a coed in Miami could have conspired with thousands of others to carry out an elaborate hoax.

Among the narratives collected during his research, Raymond Moody discovered enough similarities to construct a complete experience. While no one reports every facet of this "model," many tell of experiencing most of them.

He writes:

A man is dying and, as he reaches the point of greatest physical distress, he hears himself pronounced dead by his doctor. He begins to hear an uncomfortable noise, a loud ringing or buzzing, and at the same time feels himself moving very rapidly through a long, dark tunnel.

After this, he suddenly finds himself

outside of his own physical body, but still in the immediate physical environment, and he sees his own body from a distance, as though he is a spectator. He watches the resuscitation attempt from this unusual vantage point and is in a state of emotional upheaval.

After a while, he collects himself and becomes more accustomed to his odd condition. He notices that he still has a "body," but one of a very different nature and with very different powers from the physical body he has left behind.

Soon . . . others come to meet and to help him. He glimpses the spirits of relatives and friends who have already died, and a loving, warm spirit of a kind he has never encountered before—a being of light—appears before him. This being asks him a question, nonverbally, to make him evaluate his life and helps him along by showing him a panoramic, instantaneous playback of the major events of his life.

At some point he finds himself approaching some sort of barrier or border, apparently representing the limit between earthly life and the next life. Yet, he finds that he must go back to the earth, that time for his death has not yet come. At this point he resists, for by now he is taken up with his experiences in the afterlife and does not want to return. He is overwhelmed by intense feelings of joy, love and peace. Despite his attitude, though, he somehow reunites with his physical body and lives.

> Later he tries to tell others, but he has
> trouble doing so. In the first place, he can
> find no human words adequate to describe
> these unearthly episodes. He also finds
> that others scoff, so he stops telling other
> people. Still, the experience affects his life
> profoundly, especially his views about
> death and its relationship to life.[5]

After leaving my body, I experienced several of
these elements. I moved rapidly through a vast,
dark void; I saw my body from a distance, discovered
it wasn't my time to go, but didn't want to leave the
presence of the being of light. I felt overwhelmed by
intense feelings of joy, love and peace. Everything
appeared transparent; movement from place to
place was rapid. Communication, I discovered, is a
direct, unimpeded transfer of thoughts. My whole
life was displayed in what seemed an instant of
earthly time. Yet, despite its quickness, the review
was incredibly vivid. I, too, had the feeling of being
totally loved and accepted and that I was to be sent
back with a mission, no longer fearing death.
Although I have related my experience numerous
times, I know that my human vocabulary simply
cannot describe what I saw.

Many others report journeys similar to mine.
While some describe buzzing or roaring sounds as
they leave the body, others hear the sounds of
screaming or of crying children. Very common is the
presence of beautiful music.

A man who was freezing to death describes his
experience:

> At first, dying by freezing is very
> unpleasant. The pain sort of creeps up on
> you slowly at first, then it gets worse and

worse. I soon discovered that it was much better to lie there without moving.

Then I felt myself getting warm. It did not seem possible. But I felt just like I was inside an electric blanket in my bed. I felt good now.

The world around me became a blue-white tunnel. I felt myself starting to move toward a glowing warm light. I heard voices and music. The music was like choral music. It was very nice and relaxing. I was dead, and I felt very good. I was floating through this light blue universe.[6]

The Floating Second Body

While hearing blissful choral music, many people find themselves out of their dying bodies and floating gently and peacefully nearby.

Others, like veterinarian Robert Volgenau of Leon, New York, feel themselves floating up, accompanied by no music. He says, "I felt a wispy substance part from my body and float upward from my bed. Looking down, I saw that my body appeared to be without life."[7]

Some can direct their floating second bodies at will to other locations on Earth. Charles Redmon, "dead" from a massive stroke, recalls his experience:

My first thought was to go home—particularly since I hadn't been home for three weeks. So I glided silently out of my room at St. Luke's Hospital and floated quietly down to the parking lot outside.

I saw some people getting into a car and floated toward them. I had no idea who they were, but I asked them to drive me home. They ignored me, so I glided past them and into the back seat of their car. . . .

Then, as we approached an intersection near my home, I noticed the driver signaling a right turn. I wanted to go left, so when the car stopped at the intersection, I glided out an open window and began floating toward my home.[8]

Another man found striking evidence that his out-of-the-body episode was not an hallucination:

I found myself floating through the sky toward my home. It was a beautiful, sunny afternoon, and the trip was very pleasant.

My attention was drawn to a neighbor's yard. I saw—casually, without realizing how important it would be to me later—that he was planting two small trees. . . .

The truth hit the first day I was able to get out on crutches after being released from the hospital. I hobbled over to my neighbor's . . . and there they were! The two saplings I'd seen him plant in my "dream"! I was flabbergasted.[9]

Tunnel Vision

An almost universal characteristic of out-of-the-body phenomena is the sensation of speeding through a tunnel—also described as a vacuum, funnel, valley, well, cylinder, cave, or shapeless, dark void.

No one can say for sure when one passes through this tunnel, or if it seems to be a passageway into deeper dimensions of the other side.

People experience the tunnel at different points in a sequence of events; a few miss it altogether. Most see themselves approaching a brilliant light or an array of colored lights as they float through the dark void.

One woman said she floated "in a long shaft that seemed very narrow at first and then became wider and wider—always getting wider and with brighter and more radiant colors the farther I floated forward in the passageway."[10]

Another woman related:

> I felt myself thrust rapidly into utter, blank darkness, and I was terrified. Suddenly, I saw a tiny spot of light coming toward me. As it neared, it grew larger and larger until I could squeeze through it. I found myself standing in a desolate area spotted with rocks and surrounded by a red glow.[11]

The colors seen at the end of the tunnel are described by one traveler as "merging together in an iridescent play of tints, only to fall apart into separate hues like a bouquet of flowers opened up."[12]

The Being of Light

Virtually all who have had out-of-the-body experiences report meeting a being of light. The shining light grows larger and brighter until it finally engulfs the individual as he emerges at the other end. The being itself usually is not seen, for it is cloaked in the brightness.

Experiences with this radiance are varied. Carmene Ray of Florida was near death in the hospital. Aware of hovering over her body, she reports:

> I felt drawn almost magnetically to a blue light that was above me. As I floated closer to that magnificent glow, I could see that it looked just like the moon, and I felt myself being drawn up and behind it.
> For a minute, I hung suspended, clinging to the air with my fingertips. I knew that if I relinquished my grip, just let my fingers loosen, I would float behind that beautiful glowing moon.[13]

One man describes the light as a net:

> I was moving at high speed toward a net of great luminosity. The strands and knots where the luminous lines intersected were vibrating with a tremendous cold energy. . . . The instant I made contact with it, the vibrant luminosity increased to a blinding intensity which drained, absorbed and transformed me at the same time.[14]

Instant Replay

The encounter with the being of light often begins with a review of the person's past life. The display is multidimensional, in color, moves chronologically and extraordinarily fast. Scenes seem to come all at once, yet each is distinct and complete, with a review of the person's whole life taking place in just an instant of earthly time.

The being of light usually conducts this review, asking questions and commenting. But extreme caution must be exercised here against deception.

The life review is reported in such terms as "My entire life unreeled itself "; "Everything I had done came before me"; "I saw my life unfold before me in a procession of images."

Admiral Francis Beaufort had such a review when he nearly drowned. His story was related by the *London Daily News* in the mid-nineteenth century:

> Traveling backwards, every past incident of my life seemed to glance across my recollection in retrograde succession; not, however, in mere outline, as here stated, but the picture filled up with every minute and collateral feature.
>
> In short, the whole period of my existence seemed to be placed before me in a kind of panoramic review, and each act of it seemed to be accompanied by a consciousness of right and wrong, or by some reflection on its cause or its consequences.[15]

Not everyone feels pangs of conscience over the wrongs they have committed. Some report that the being of light doesn't seem overly concerned with the review. The being apparently prefers the role of an impartial observer during the review, usually wrapping things up with some advice for the subject on learning to love more and gathering more knowledge when he returns to life.[16]

Escorts into the Beyond

Many of those traveling to the other side encounter "dead" relatives or other entities who help them on their journey. According to

parapsychologist Dr. Karlis Osis, approximately
eighty percent of those having near-death
experiences have such encounters. Typical is the
story of an eleven-year-old girl with a congenital
heart defect:

> She was having another bad episode with
> her heart, and said that she saw her mother
> in a pretty white dress and that her mother
> had one just like it for her. She was very
> happy and smiling, and told me to let her
> get up and go over there—her mother was
> ready to take her on a trip.
>
> The vision lasted for half an hour. It left
> the girl serene and peaceful until her death
> four hours later. The unusual part of this
> case is that the girl never knew her mother,
> who had died when giving birth to her.[17]

Another example is that of Judith Reeves, a
retired schoolteacher who underwent a critical
operation for a ruptured intestine.
She reports:

> Two heavenly white angels came to me.
> They settled on each side of my shoulders
> and quietly and gently lifted my spirit from
> my pain-wracked body and glided away
> with me.
>
> We moved over dark valleys, high
> mountains and the seas. I felt no fear—only
> complete peace and contentment.
>
> Suddenly, there appeared the most
> glorious light, unlike anything I'd ever
> seen. It seemed as though a celestial
> city—all white and gleaming—was

suspended in the sky, surrounded by a magnificent golden light.

And there in the doorway of this beautiful city stood my mother who'd died 50 years before, her arms open wide to receive me.

All her lines of age had slipped from her face. She looked like a very young woman. There was no pain on her face as there'd been when I'd last seen her—just an indescribable smile of happiness.[18]

Encounters with a death angel are sometimes reported. The entity has been identified as a hooded, faceless messenger of death. One woman described it this way:

Some time while in my coma, I suddenly became aware of a black, hooded figure floating over my bed, with its cape swaying.

There was no face inside the hood, but I heard a voice softly say: "Come, it is time to go." Then I became aware of two other figures beside the hooded messenger—my mother and an older sister.

Before I could say anything, my mother spoke to the hooded form: "No, she's not ready yet." Then, without warning, my mother and sister (who had been dead for many years) disappeared.

The hooded figure circled above my bed once, appeared to look at me thoughtfully . . . and then it quietly disappeared also.

Although I did not see an angel of death, its

presence must have been in the hospital room when I died. On three occasions grim darkness entered my room, appearing like a black wall, and as it spread from the left side of my bed, the light began to vanish from the right. It appeared death and life were waging a battle. Finally the darkness prevailed, and I began my rapid flight beyond.

Garden of Peace

Many visit a realm of tranquil gardens. Often, the relatives they meet are part of this pastoral environment.

After his heart attack, French movie actor Daniel Gélin reported seeing "a rose-colored world, a sort of fairy garden filled with wonderful flowers."[19]

Another man gazed upon a meadow that "went on forever" and said:

> I saw dense forests in the far distance. Both the meadow and the forests were filled with all kinds of animals . . . playing together.
> The only word I seem to be able to use to talk about that place is "beautiful." It was much more than that word will ever reveal.[20]

Coming Back

Ultimately, the tranquil scenes have given way to a wrenching return to the physical body. This is as varied an experience as the departure. The return is so rapid most people do not remember it. My first recollection of reentry is that my body suddenly felt cold, and I opened my eyes and smiled at one of the nurses!

Those who do remember their return have various

ways of describing it. Some felt jerked from the beyond. Others say they fell like dead weights back into their bodies, received a jolt as spirit and body merged, were sucked again through a dark tunnel, or were squeezed back into the body.

While attending a service one evening in the mid-1950s at Central Bible College in Springfield, Missouri, student Sally Lansdowne suddenly found herself floating above her body. Gazing at her praying form in a seat below, Sally sensed herself rising slowly toward the high ceiling of the auditorium.

In fear she cried, "No, Lord!" The descent to her body was immediate but slow. "Upon reentry I felt squeezed into my chest," she recalls. "And I sensed a tremendous heat on my shoulder as though an invisible presence was standing behind me."

According to Dr. Paul Becker, a German internal medicine specialist, many are disappointed when they have to come back. "It hurt them," he observes. "They knew they were coming back to a body filled with pain, to diseases like cancer. . . . They all said dying is nicer and better than they ever thought it would be."[21]

One woman says, "My spirit had trouble returning to my body—as though there had been some mix-up in time. I wondered if my body had received so much damage already that I wouldn't want to return to it."[22]

Reports indicate that reentry not only occurs through the chest, but often through the head and sometimes the feet.

The Silver Cord
One other out-of-the-body characteristic should be discussed: the cord which links the physical and

spiritual bodies.

Many cite the Bible as an initial reference to this phenomenon. In Ecclesiastes 12:6, the Preacher describes a man going to his death—the time when "the silver cord be loosed" and the body returns to dust, while "the spirit shall return unto God who gave it."

From this reference some conclude that the cord connects the spiritual entity to the physical body, and it remains connected as long as the individual is meant to return to the time-space world. While I was unaware of this cord during my journey out of the body, many have noticed theirs.

Parapsychologists bear witness to the cord. Should it be snapped inadvertently, they say, the spirit would be left permanently on the other side. This is but one of the many dangers facing those who journey out of the body at will.

What is the cord like? It has been described as a chain, strand, tape, thread, ribbon or long neck. Some see it as a shaft of light, often pulsating with a vibrant energy. Others detect a number of fine threads making up a single strand, floating like a cobweb.[23]

It is variously seen as being attached to the skull, the back of the neck, the stomach, or between the shoulder blades. Monroe describes his discovery of the silver cord in one experiment:

> I reached around my head to see if I could feel it coming out the front, top, or back of my head. As I reached the back of my head, my hand brushed against something and I felt behind me with both hands.
>
> Whatever it was extended out from a spot in my back directly between my

shoulder blades, as nearly as I felt the base,
and it felt exactly like the spread out roots
of a tree radiating out from the basic trunk.
It formed into a "cord," if you can call a
two-inch-thick cable a "cord." It was
hanging loosely, and I could feel its texture
very definitely. It was body-warm to the
touch and seemed to be composed of
hundreds (perhaps thousands) of
tendonlike strands packed neatly together,
but not twisted or spiraled. It was flexible
and seemed to have no skin covering.[24]

The mystic Yram says, "The extent to which this
cord can stretch seems to be limitless, and it
resembles the trail of a rocket as it soars into space.
Where the cord joins the [spirit] double it consists of
thousands of very fine, elastic threads, which seem
to suck the double into them."[25]

Travelers to the next dimension report an
intimate connection between the physical and
spiritual bodies through the silver strand, like an
umbilical cord between mother and baby. Present
whether the traveler is near death or on an occult
exploration of other planes, the connecting thread
reveals the tenuous hold one has on life. Damage to
the cord or one's spirit double means death to the
physical body. And such damage can occur all too
easily in the unknown regions of the other side.

Depth of Experience

Many studies show that the extent to which one
experiences the other side depends on whether one
was "dead" or "near dead" and for how long this
condition lasted. Moody says, "Persons who were
'dead' seemed to report more florid, complete ex-

periences than those who only came close to death, and those who were 'dead' for a longer period go deeper than those who were 'dead' for a shorter time."[26]

Perhaps this accounts for the fact that very few see the realities of Heaven or Hell and live to tell it. Moody claims that in all the reports he has gathered, "not one person has described pearly gates, golden streets and winged, harp-playing angels, or a hell of flames and demons with pitchforks."[27]

Quest for Cosmic Awareness

With increasing curiosity, many are seeking ways to enter the beyond, hoping to return with a greater cosmic awareness. In the process a fascinating phenomenon is captivating the imagination of housewives, children, teachers, secretaries, businessmen and researchers. Psychics and parapsychologists are uncovering frightening secrets in their strange experiments.

4

Soul-Hopping in the Beyond

John Mittle of Kempton, Pennsylvania, awoke one morning and bounced down the stairs to make breakfast. When he tried to plug in the coffeepot, his hand went right through the cord!

Realizing what had happened, he reluctantly returned to his physical body, still lying in bed.

About the time Pioneer 10 was scheduled to pass Jupiter, psychics Ingo Swann and Harold Sherman took a 600-million-mile astral flight to that planet. The next day their observations of Jupiter's colors, landscapes, atmosphere and other conditions were filed with astrophysicists. Although closely paralleling Pioneer 10 data, their report was challenged.

To demonstrate their capabilities, Swann and Sherman agreed to another out-of-the-body experiment. Mariner 10 soon would pass Mercury and radio its data back to Earth. The psychics offered to project themselves to that planet and report their discoveries before the spacecraft reached its destination.

Scientists had contended that Mercury had

neither atmosphere nor magnetic field, but each psychic reported a thin atmosphere and a magnetic field. Mariner 10 confirmed this within the month.

Swann has astounded scientists with other mind-boggling feats that he claims to accomplish through out-of-body travel performed at will. He not only has the uncanny ability to describe objects hidden out of sight, but can go to any location on the globe, given its longitude and latitude, and correctly sketch mountains, rivers, roads, and buildings just as they are at that spot.

At age sixteen, Erich Von Daniken, author of the controversial bestseller, *Chariots of the Gods*, was recovering in bed from an illness.

Without warning, he recalls, "I could see my body below me, motionless on the bed. I was detached, apart, being swept into something I did not understand."

In later years, Von Daniken discovered he could leave his body at will and become part of another dimension in which the past, present, and future are one.

Feeling drowsy one afternoon, Michael Brod of Lindenhurst, New York, stretched out on his bed, eyes closed for a nap. All at once he felt wide awake and in the grip of paralysis. Lying on his back, arms by his side, Brod forced himself to sit up.

"I had the absolute sensation that I had sat up out of my body, with my legs still extended in front of me," he explains. "I remained like this for some time. I was fully able to perceive things in the room; everything had an unusual glow to it."

Shortly after lying back down, he had the sensation of awakening from sleep and was able to move freely. This experience occurred many times during the following years. One night, while in this awakened but paralyzed state, he forced himself to sit up, but suddenly began to float around the room, coming very close to the ceiling. In surprise, he willed himself back to the bed and into his body.

Later he discovered he could have willed himself to almost any place he had chosen.

When British novelist William Gerhardi reached out to turn on the bedside light as usual one night, he felt nothing. Suddenly wide awake, he realized he was floating above his own body on the bed.

"To my utter astonishment, a broad cable of light at the back of me illuminated the face on the pillow, as if attached to the brow of the sleeper," Gerhardi recounts.

"The sleeper was myself, not dead, but breathing peacefully . . . and here was I, outside it, watching it with a thrill of joy and fear.

"There was this uncanny tape of light between us like an umbilical cord, by means of which the body on the bed was kept breathing while its mold wandered about the flat through space which seemed dense as water."

Having a headache one day, German Fräulein Sophie Swoboda lay down on her bedroom sofa to rest. Awakening from a deep sleep, she saw her mother quietly leave the room. Headache gone and feeling light as a feather, Sophie followed her into the living room, watching as she sat down and began to knit. Miss Swoboda's father was reading aloud from a book.

Surprised that neither parent paid any attention to her, Sophie returned to her bedroom. She was startled by the sight of her body sleeping on the sofa, looking much like a pale corpse. Instantly, she was hurled back into it.

Later Sophie repeated word for word the text of

the book her father had been reading, as well as her parents' conversation.

What is this strange phenomenon? Is it a dream, or can a person's spirit actually depart the body at times other than death or near-death?

What strange fascination is enticing thousands to momentarily forsake their bodies and visit the invisible realms of the unknown?

What mysterious secret have these people uncovered, enabling them to go anywhere unhindered and undetected, observing persons, actions and events, then returning to their physical bodies with full memory of the trip?

What dangers lurk in afterworld planes, prompting even occultists to give warnings about travel to these realms?

Like Flicking a Switch

The phenomenon of out-of-the-body travel is a relatively common occurrence today. Often after reliving my own experience before audiences, I am told by many of my listeners that they, too, have seen the other side.

Journeys to the world beyond are being reported not only by the dying and those who have died and returned to tell it, but by no-nonsense businessmen, housewives, and young people.

In occult circles the ability to slip out of one's physical wrapper—the body—and travel from this dimension within spiritual planes is called astral projection. This is one of the most desired achievements in the occult and has captivated many people, often to a greater extent than they ever wished to be. Because the phenomenon is not usually induced by physical trauma or drugs, it is distinguishable from the out-of-the-body experiences of the dead and dying.

Astral projection is the willful desire and effort of an individual to disconnect some part of his consciousness from his physical body in order to experience life in a new form and an altered state. In astral projection an ethereal body, along with what could be called the mind or understanding, is able to separate from the physical body and operate independently of it. One retains normal faculties, but also exercises a type of heightened sensory awareness.

With these new senses, one experiences things differently and at times more directly and intimately than with the physical senses. Objects and thought forms appear to the mind's eye differently than in normal physical perception.

In astral projection, an individual perceives a portion of his environment impossible to see from the location of his body. Because he still possesses his normal consciousness, the individual also knows at the time that the experience is real.

Usually, the astral projection is triggered by a variety of meditation techniques, although it can occur spontaneously, sometimes uncontrollably, to people who have become unusually sensitive to other-world life.

The techniques for astral projection may seem complicated, but separating from the body is easy—if you know how and can completely relax mind and body. One Portland, Oregon, housewife says, "I found an astral projection as easy to accomplish as flicking on a light switch. This, of course, was after I had familiarized myself with the techniques involved."[1]

Dream or Reality

Psychics believe astral projections happen to everyone sometime in their lives—while sleeping or in an unconscious state. Most of these experiences, they say, are not remembered upon awakening.

Think back to the time you had an unusually vivid dream. Was it really a dream, or were you traveling in your astral body to another dimension and another time? While a dream is a symbolic occurrence in which the actors and scenery are often exaggerated, the astral flight takes one's soul to realms as real as the physical world. Many have returned with evidence to prove this point.

In 1934, a man made four astral trips from his apartment in Great Neck, Long Island, New York, to the home of his in-laws in Mt. Rainier, Maryland, 240 miles away. Here is his account of one projection:

> I found myself viewing their three-story frame house in Mt. Rainier from an altitude of seemingly a hundred or so feet. I observed the area for a long moment, then I was in their kitchen, perfectly seeing and hearing my wife, her mother, and sister.
>
> Mother-in-law was finishing drying some utensils at the kitchen sink and placing them in their storage places; sister-in-law Hazel and my wife were seated opposite each other at the large table in the oversized breakfast nook, which was the east portion of the large kitchen.
>
> Hazel suggested making up another batch of scrapple; my wife enthusiastically agreed to the project; mother-in-law concurred. Then they began busying themselves with utensils and condiments.

Feeling tired, he returned to his body in Long Island. The following weekend, the man visited his mother-in-law and described the family's activities accurately. While the mother-in-law admitted a strong feeling of his presence in the room at the time of his projection trip, his wife and sister-in-law remained unimpressed by his prior knowledge of the scrapple-making.[2]

On May 28, 1961, Carol Hales of Quartz Hills, California, saw a vision of the agonized face of her friend Jaime Palmer in the branches of a tall eucalyptus tree in her yard, as though pleading for help. The image of Miss Palmer faded away, and Carol rushed to the telephone to call her. Receiving no answer, Carol was desperate. She lay on her bed and projected herself to Jaime's house. In an instant, she found herself entering Jaime's bedroom from the balcony, discovering her almost unconscious on the bed.

Carol moved to the bedside and laid her hand upon Jaime's forehead. Realizing she had to get help fast, Carol returned to the balcony, floated over the railing, and drifted slowly down to the garden. Passing one of the orange trees, she wrapped her fingers around a piece of foliage and projected onward to her own bed ten miles away. Returning to her body, she found a sprig of bright green in her hand from an orange tree. Since no such trees grew near her home, she knew without a doubt that what had just happened was no dream.

Carol immediately called her good friend and physician, Dr. Marion J. Dakin, who sped to Jaime's house with a nurse. They found her desperately ill. Jaime was rushed to Santa Monica Hospital, where an exceptionally large gallstone was removed.

"If my experience was merely a dream," Miss

Hales asks, "then where did I get the foliage from an orange tree? And how did I know of Jaime's desperate need?"[3]

Another account is given by a businessman in his mid-thirties who tells how he traveled in an astral body to a friend's birthday party when he was eight years old. As he relates the incident:

It was around eight o'clock at night, and I was home wishing that I could be at my best friend's house where he was having his birthday party. My mother had kept me home that night since I had gotten sick. . . .

I was still thinking hard about the party I was missing when I felt wide awake. All at once I drifted out of my body. I remember the weightless feeling. I felt free of restrictions. I remember the events vividly. I had to look down to see the little boy's body lying there on the bed, and I knew at once it was my body!

I drifted up toward the ceiling like a balloon. . . . I don't know how I did it, but I could float from one corner of the room to the next. I thought about my friend's party, and I suddenly found myself going through my door—not opening it, but through it. The next thing that I knew, I was drifting toward the front door of my friend's house. I went through the door. . . . .

Everyone there was really having a good time. My friend was there, and I tried getting his attention by calling out to him. But he did not hear me nor did he see me. I heard Jim (his friend) talking to one stranger. "I have seen you before at school, but I didn't know we were neighbors." The stranger answered, "We only moved in last month from Dallas, and I don't get out much. I'm Alan."

The boy drifted around the room for a time, playing games with his ability to pass through people and objects until the voice of his mother called from a distance.

"Ralph, Ralph, wake up." The voice was worried, and I suddenly realized that it belonged to my mother. Instantly I was back in my body.

It was a week later at school that I was talking to my friend Jim. I told him about the party and said, "I dreamed that you were talking to this new guy, and he was telling you that he had just moved into the neighborhood from Dallas. He didn't get to go out much and that was the reason that you didn't know that he was your neighbor."

Jim was a little startled at first because he said that that was right. My friend thought someone who was at the party told me about Alan. But this wasn't true. No one told me about anything that happened at the party. I had not spoken to anyone before meeting Jim at school.[4]

Significant Patterns
In recent years, astral projection has joined mental telepathy and other psychic phenomena in the laboratory. The files of psychics, researchers

and scientists contain thousands of out-of-the-body cases that are alike in essential patterns but different in details.

In projections from either a sleeping or waking state, the astral or second body moves out of its physical shell, glides around the room, floats to the ceiling or travels great distances, sometimes around the world.

A Dr. Ostby once decided to project to a certain man in Chicago, far from his own home. In the astral plane, however, he sensed that the man was now living in California, but he didn't know where.

"Almost instantaneously Dr. Ostby found himself in a strange town in California and in front of a bungalow. He went inside and saw the man, learning that he was a dope addict," writes Herbert Greenhouse in *The Astral Journey*. "Later, Dr. Ostby secured photographs of the man and the bungalow he was living in, both exactly as he had seen them in his astral body. All other items checked out, including the fact that the man was taking dope."[5]

Soul travelers may find themselves in unfamiliar or unreal surroundings and encounter shadowy figures moving through mist or fog. Sometimes the setting can be heavenly, bathed in brilliant light and vivid colors.[6]

Many astral projections have carried experimenters forward or backward in time. One psychic reported visits to cities a thousand years in the future. He claims to be working on a system for bringing back some real knowledge from these trips.[7]

Dr. Robert Crookall, a psychologist who conducts extensive psychical research, noted that the astral body is not completely detached from its physical shell. As in death and near-death experiences, a silver cord connects the body and its astral double.[8]

Other patterns are detectable. Unaffected by gravity, astral travelers can speed instantly and automatically anywhere in the world they choose, often returning with such psychic abilities as telepathy, clairvoyance and foreknowledge.

Even in the separation process similarities exist. One researcher makes this observation:

> Watch for the following sequence that is often part of the process: the physical body falls into a trancelike, frequently cataleptic state just before or after projection; there is a momentary blackout just before the bodies separate; the second body rises to a horizontal position above the physical body, then uprights itself; the astral projector looks back and sees his physical body lying on the bed or relaxing in a chair where he left it; the projector sees a cordlike connection between the two bodies; the projector returns to his physical body the same way he left it, with the steps reversed.
>
> The second body may also rotate out of the physical body in a spiral motion and return the same way. The second body generally feels very light, usually weightless, and sometimes gives off a glow that may illuminate a dark room.[9]

The separation process can happen slowly or with lightning speed, catching the projector by surprise. Sometimes an individual may experience the sensation of being sucked up violently as by a whirlwind. In the latter case, immediate and conscious contact with astral realms is reached. No visions or sensations accompany projection by whirlwind. Instead, the traveler is transported on "a wind of ether," also described as a magnetic current, toward an unknown destination. A sense of tremendous speed and the sounding of a deafening, howling tempest accompanies one's flight, and on some occasions a white, luminous cloud has been seen trailing the spirit body.[10]

Nothing New

Astral projection is not a modern phenomenon. The ancient Chinese meditated to achieve astral travel, and out-of-the-body processes familiar to investigators are engraved on some Chinese seventeenth-century wooden tablets. Many cultures of the past mention the spirit body—Hindu, Buddhist, Egyptian, Indian, Greek, British and Roman.

The Roman philosopher Apuleius claims to have gone on an astral journey as part of the initiation ceremony into the Mysteries of Isis, the Egyptian goddess. The objective was to release his spirit through self-hypnosis and ritual and finally come to know what paradise is like.

The *Tibetan Book of the Dead* teaches that the departed soul wanders about a Hades-like region for three days before the separation of the physical and astral bodies is complete. The Tibetans also traveled astrally before death, visiting places on Earth or going to paradise and purgatory."[11]

Throughout history and wherever psychics have flourished, accounts of astral travel abound.

Motivations

The desire to leave the body through astral projection usually comes about in one of three ways. First, one has an out-of-the-body experience, finds it pleasurable, and tries to repeat it. Second, hearing that such an experience is possible, many are led to undertake some form of occult discipline to achieve it. Third, many believe it is a method by which they can attain a better and fuller life, arriving ideally at the fulfillment of the true purpose of existence: spiritual regeneration.

Engrossed in occult disciplines for more than twenty years, ex-psychic Michael Brod says, "When I began these studies, I had already rejected the traditional teachings of Judaism concerning God, and I endeavored to devise a method to establish an intimate and fulfilling relationship with God on my own. Within the view that I had, I rejected the concept of sin and accepted the idea that I would be justified by my experience.

"To my view, my righteousness lay in reaching beyond the natural realm of experience into the supernatural, where I believed I would experience true godliness. I did not desire power of any kind for itself, but rather desired a supernatural intervention which would have the power to transform my life. I was living under these concepts and under this influence when I had my first out-of-the-body experience."

Frightening Encounters

The soul traveler can have some unpleasant surprises.

Says Yram, "During one experiment, when I had used more effort than usual to project myself, I was hardly out of my body when I received a terrific slap in the face without being able to find whence it came.

"Another time I was scarcely out of my body when I began to turn on my own axis, like looping the loop, which was not at all pleasant. A further example, even more unpleasant, was . . . that day . . . I became aware of an intense disorganization in my astral body. I had a feeling of having every atom broken to pieces."

Yram even reports problems awaiting the projector after return to his physical body: "Once I had trouble with an unreasonable fear . . . the beating of my heart was almost imperceptible and my limbs would not obey my will." On another occasion, he was nearly run over. "No longer having full control over my body, I still had the feeling of walking on air. On stepping off the tram it seemed as if a chasm were opening at my feet, and I reacted violently in order to keep my balance."[12]

Warnings by Psychics

The pursuit of out-of-the-body travel can not only lead one into the occult, but can bring the explorer to a world of satanic influence and control.

The psychic, Ophiel, warns, "I would not plan on contacting your departed relatives on the next plane by the use of these projection methods I am teaching. It is not that you would be barred by entities there, but the road there is beset with strange difficulties, and things are much different on that plane than what the world thinks it is. It has something to do with the real separation that comes with death that makes your live projections act very strange in that plane-place."[13]

Many dangers threaten both the departed spirit and the vacated body. While the process of separation may be as easy as "flicking a light switch" once the technique is learned, trying to stop this ability could be like trying to put a rebellious genie back into its bottle. "The astral body," says psychic Harold Sherman, "seems to have a will of its own."[14]

In what state is the body during a projection? Sherman's answer is typical of the response by other experts in the field:

> Sleep has been described, by men and women who have been able to leave the physical body and travel about, as the little sister of death. This is because, in order for the soul or entity to depart from the flesh house in which it resides during life on Earth, it must leave the physical form in a deep cataleptic state closely resembling death.[15]

What is startling in the light of this observation is his answer to the question, *Is there any danger of the physical body being occupied by a disincarnate entity while the soul is on a journey*? "In the early stages of development this seems possible," he warns. [16]

If the threat of bodily invasion by evil beings of the other dimension exists, is it possible for an astral traveler to accidentally find himself in the body of another person—living or dead—upon reentry?

A prominent businessman in an eastern state, whom Sherman calls Robert Penn, gives this frightening account:

> Temporarily, unknowingly, one time I entered the body of a man who had just died. He was in a hospital, and I was able to prove this out by checking with doctors and describing to them what had taken place in the patient's room at the time of his demise, and finding myself in his body.
>
> You can be sure I got out of it as quickly

as possible, and back into my own body, in my home, several miles away!

Two other times I entered the body of a person who seemed to be in a nightclub, possibly under the effect of drugs. I found myself smoking. I was not conscious of the personality or identity; it may have been temporarily off somewhere.

Considered to be one of the foremost adventurers into realms beyond the physical, Penn warns of the risks in astral projection:

Once you have become adept at leaving your body, you often do it in your sleep, and have little choice. I suppose if you stayed out overlong, something might happen to your physical body. It could get too cold, aching in the joints. The body slows up physiologically when you are away from it.

During my earlier experiments, I felt there might be danger of some other entity taking over my body while I was out. There was a debilitation risk.

Now an out-of-body experience is quite refreshing. I become so engrossed with the bigger reality where I am, I'm sometimes tempted to stay—to become a "mental dropout"—and I have to watch that.[17]

Another risk is an encounter with evil beings. Penn admits "low entities tried to attack me," and describes his experiences as frightening and horrifying.

Robert Monroe, who teaches techniques for leaving the body, frequently encounters spirit-world

entities. One of the greatest mysteries in his
experiments is the help he has received from a being
or group of beings on the other side.

Monroe admits he doesn't know whether such
helpers are guardian angels, and he is puzzled as to
why they are helping. "They do not always respond
when I need help. . . . Mental anguish and
screaming have sometimes brought one of them.
More often, they help me when I do not ask for help.
They are rarely 'friendly' in the sense that we
understand the term. Yet there is a definite sense of
understanding, knowledge, and purposefulness in
their actions toward me."[18]

On one occasion he was escorted by two of his
helpers to a seance in a New York apartment. Here
is his account of what took place:

> After a normal evening at home, my wife
> and I went up to bed around eleven-thirty.
> My wife fell asleep almost immediately. As
> I lay there, evidently deeply relaxed and
> possibly half-asleep, I suddenly felt that
> "walking over your grave" coldness, and
> the hairs on the back of my neck started to
> rise.
>
> I looked across the half-darkened room,
> fearful yet utterly fascinated. I don't know
> what I expected, but standing in the
> doorway leading from the hall was a white
> ghost-like figure. It actually looked like the
> traditional figure of a ghost—some six feet
> tall . . . with a flowing sheetlike material
> draping it from its head to the floor. One
> hand was reaching out and holding onto the
> door jamb.
>
> I was completely frightened, and I had
> no chance to connect the figure with

anything I had done. The moment it began to move toward me, I cringed in half terror and at the same time felt I had to see what it was. Almost immediately, I felt hands placed over my eyes so I couldn't see.

Then someone took hold of my upper arms, gently, and I moved up out of the bed. Immediately, there was a quick sense of movement and we (I then felt there were two of them, one on each side) were suddenly over a small room, as if we were looking down on it from the ceiling. In the room below were four women. I looked at the two beings on each side of me. One was a blond male, the other dark-haired, almost oriental. Both seemed to be quite young, in their early twenties. They were smiling at me.

I spoke to them . . . then I floated down to the only empty chair and sat down in it. A tall, large woman in a dark suit sat opposite me. A woman in what looked like an ankle-length white robe sat next to me. The other two were indistinct. A woman's voice asked if I would remember that I had been there, and I assured her that I certainly would.

Then one of the women (the one in the dark suit) came over and swung over the side of my chair, and draped herself right on top of me! I didn't feel her weight, but for some reason, she got up suddenly. There was laughter. Evidently, the contact with the woman who sat on top of me had altered things. Just at that moment, I heard a male voice say, "I think he's been away long enough; we'd better take him back. Almost instantly, I was back lying in my bed.[19]

Monroe adds a further perspective to the frightening encounters of the astral plane, which he identifies as Locale II. He mentions a layer of some kind which one must pass through in the part of Locale II closest to the here-and-now. "It is a gray-black hungry ocean where the slightest motion attracts nibbling and tormenting beings," he says. "It is as if you are the bait dangling in this vast sea. If you move slowly and do not react to the curious 'fish' who come to investigate, you pass through without much incident. Move violently and fight back, then more excited denizens come rushing in to bite, pull, push, and shove.

"Could this be the borders of Hell?" he asks. "It is easy to conclude that a momentary penetration of this nearby layer would bring demons and devils to mind as the chief inhabitants. They seem subhuman, yet have an evident ability to act and think independently."

Who, or what, are they? "I don't know," Monroe admits. "I haven't taken the trouble to stay there long enough to find out!" In many of his astral journeys, he concedes, "some of the resulting destinations have had all the aspects of Hell to me."[20]

On another occasion, as psychic Monroe was separating from his physical body, he felt something climb on his back. He vainly tried to rid himself of the entities clinging like leeches to his astral body. After a vicious struggle, he managed to yank the creatures off his back. Here is an excerpt from his startling account:

> Then . . . I floated over into the center
> of the office, holding one in each hand,
> screaming for help. I got a good look at

each, and as I looked, each turned into a good facsimile of one of my two daughters! I seemed to know immediately that this was a deliberate camouflage on their parts to create emotional confusion in me and call upon my love for my daughters to prevent my doing more to them.

The moment I realized the trick, the two no longer appeared to be my daughters. Desperate for a solution, I thought about fire, and this seemed to help a little. However, I got the impression that they were both amused, as if there was nothing I could do to harm them. By this time, I was sobbing for help.

Then Monroe saw a man approaching, wearing a dark robe that extended down to his ankles. After observing the scene for a long moment, he picked up the little beings, cradled one in each arm and left. Sobbing his thanks, Monroe reentered his body and looked around. The room was empty.[21]

Volumes can be written on the astral plane perils awaiting intruders from the space-time world. Even Buddha was aware of the phenomenon and sternly warned his followers not to practice it.[22]

While Dr. Crookall contends that astral projections are genuine experiences, he doesn't recommend indiscriminate attempts to project, either. "Projections may come unbidden when one is not ready," he says. "If forced, there may be highly undesirable results." He warns, "No one who is not mentally and emotionally stable and controlled should try to obtain any psychical experience, for 'fools rush in where angels fear to tread.'"[23]

An example of this is cited by the ASPR's Dr. Osis. At one time during his research into out-of-the-body phenomena, he conducted experiments with a gifted Baltimore resident. With his body remaining in Baltimore, the man would travel to Osis's New York office and later describe target objects that were left on top of the desk.

But Osis is quick to note that his friend was soon afterward admitted to a mental hospital.

"He lost conscious control over his out-of-body travel," Osis explains. "He kept 'popping' out of his body all the time. Once he called collect from the hospital and asked, 'Fly with me again.' I got scared after that telephone call. I quit working with him. I haven't tried any experiments involving out-of-the-body experiences since that time."[24]

Another astral adventurer, Oliver Fox, admonishes, "We are dealing with what is essentially a mental exercise or process, and it is easily conceivable that an ill-balanced mind, lacking in self-control, might become temporarily or even permanently deranged." The possible dangers that Fox foresees include heart failure or insanity arising from shock, premature death, temporary derangement, cerebral hemorrhage, severance of the silver cord (which means death) repercussions upon the physical body caused by injuries to the astral double, and demon possession.[25]

Leaving the body to go soul-hopping through astral worlds is indeed dangerous, for the possibility exists that one may not be able to get back.

Robert Antoszczyk, a twenty-nine-year-old yoga instructor, was found dead in his room on June 3, 1975, in a meditation position. Medical examiners could find no reason for his death.

On June 1, Antoszczyk had entered his room, telling friends not to disturb him. A few days earlier he had told an astrologer friend that he hoped to project to the other side over the weekend. Some of the young man's friends believe Antosczcyk decided not to return to his body because his soul found a better life.

Did Antosczcyk decide to stay on the other side? Or did he enter such a deep trance as he meditated that his heart slowed down, starving his brain of life-supporting blood?

As a former astral projector, Michael Brod may have a clue. Forms of imprisonment have been experienced in the beyond in which soul travelers have been held captive by entities seeking to hinder their return to the physical body.

"In each instance, the inability to return to the body would have caused the death of the astral projector," Brod observes. "Books on astral projection usually give a detailed description of what to do if one finds himself trapped in the astral world. Each book warns the practitioner that the inability to return to the physical body when opposed by evil beings will result in death. These precautions may only be the insidious work of demon spirits, causing anguish in the minds of occult practitioners, but if valid, it is evident that there are two different worlds in which out-of-the-body experiences can occur. Therefore, the person who practices astral projection risks not only demonic influence but physical death."

Question for Christians

Can Christians travel in the next dimension, and should they search for the key unlocking the door to the other side? I wonder if the powers and capabilities of the supernatural realm are neutral, and if the Christian has the option to use such powers. The evidence shows astral projection to be a dangerous occult practice.

Christians of notable reputation have traveled

beyond and returned. A spontaneous out-of-the-body episode is not of itself occultic. Holding the key to other dimensions, God can at His own prerogative summon us beyond. I have cited such cases in earlier pages. It is rather the practice of projection to satisfy one's own fascinations and curiosity that propels the individual into Satan's territory.

All of man's involvement with the supernatural, his pursuit of secret knowledge, is conditioned and controlled by what God considers lawful, since He has chosen to retain certain knowledge for Himself.

Even Adam's quest for knowledge was conditioned by God. Adam ate the mysterious fruit of the tree of the knowledge of good and evil, but he had been forbidden to do so. We can conclude that, while a power or capability may enable a person to experience the unknown, it is clearly not always God's will for him to do so.

The emergence of hundreds of sects and philosophical groups which promise unique means of self-purification and self-unfolding, culminating in so-called righteousness, is evidence of the extent of man's delusion in believing he can attain salvation by his own efforts or through some other-world experience.

Most sects and occult groups conceive of a neutral power or universal force accessible to all. While God is considered the creator of the neutral power, the belief is that this universal force working in one's life produces the righteousness God demands.

By applying the methods of discipline or meditation taught by their organizations, these groups say, the force will operate in the practitioner's life.

Many groups claim also that they are in contact

with supernatural beings who will aid the practitioner in his efforts to achieve spiritual fulfillment, and, as an outcome, sinlessness. Others claim that a change in one's thinking pattern will harness this neutral power for one's benefit. Although many of these groups use biblical quotations to support their beliefs, they have clearly bypassed the cross of Christ as the only means to attain salvation.

When Adam sinned, he lost his original state of purity. Whatever he retained of his powers, his capabilities were insufficient to reinstate his former sinlessness. Knowing this, God made provision for Adam, establishing a way for the broken relationship between man and God to be restored. Ultimately, Christ would travel from the other side to His physical world and offer Himself once and for all as a sacrifice, thus saving mankind from destruction and reestablishing communication between the physical and spiritual planes. God has told man to seek Him on these terms, rather than by any methods we may have invented.

Other-world realities have become shrouded by man's fallen nature. In this respect we have become infants of the universe, having lost the ability to comprehend dimensions of the spirit. Without the protection and guidance of God, those who venture beyond are at the mercy of whoever and whatever is out there.

Law of the Astral

Astral realms are governed by strict laws. Some of these are recorded in the Bible. Seeking supernatural knowledge through astral projection, which falls under the category of witchcraft, is condemned as unlawful in Deuteronomy 18:10-12.

The practice of witchcraft and sorcery in their more esoteric forms relies heavily on and seeks out-of-the-body experience through astral projection.[26] This has given rise to the belief that witches fly, which they do in the astral world. Clearly, such is not a lawful pursuit for a Christian.

Although Jesus had an out-of-the-body experience at His death, returning from the beyond at His resurrection, there is no evidence that He practiced astral projection. While out-of-the-body phenomena were experienced by some individuals mentioned in the Bible, none of them actively sought it. Several incidents of "translation" are recorded, in which the individual's physical body was transported to a far removed location in an instant of time.[27] But in each instance, an act of God was involved. Astral projection is not God's intention for His followers.

Because attempts at astral projection inevitably lead one into the occult, we should be warned. As long as God initiates our supernatural experiences, we can be sure we are in good hands.

5

Perils of Parallel Planes

Around the globe secret doors open into mysterious passageways to other worlds. At least one of these worlds is inhabited.

Existing somewhere on the other side is a non-material locale populated by intelligent entities with whom communication is possible.

Beneath the ocean in the Bermuda Triangle lies an ancient underwater civilization. Such subterranean life might explain why observers have seen numerous UFOs in that area.

Perhaps these and other intriguing theories would unveil the enigmas of spiritual phenomena.

Christian writers are beginning to explore the question of whether such theories could be correct. Two researchers into the parallel-world theory say, "There is overwhelming biblical evidence of a spiritual and supernatural world that is not perceptible to our senses, yet it moves parallel to our material existence and affects us profoundly. The parallel world is the abode of spirits. We believe entities in the parallel world are intruding into the material realm, and we are seeing the effects in a world rapidly moving toward a period of tremendous geological, social, political, and religious upheaval."[1]

John Weldon, in *UFOs: What on Earth Is Happening?*, discusses this concept:

> It is high time that we all realize that there exists a spiritual—supernatural, invisible, whatever concept you prefer—world. This world, not perceptible by our senses, moves along a parallel to our earthly existence and affects us profoundly all the time.
>
> This parallel world . . . is a very full world, occupied by a variety of beings and entities, rather like the world we can see.
>
> The Bible characterizes the spiritual world as experiencing ongoing warfare on the angelic level—the very sons of God are in contention. We see it clearly in the painful experiences of Job, and we will see it objectively revealed in the Tribulation to come.[2]

While the descriptions of the Christian and occult astral realms often differ, similarities exist. Although rooted in the occult, could an element of truth be found in the non-Christian theories? Psychic accounts of the world beyond resemble in some respects what the Bible teaches.

One theory is offered as a solution to the mysterious disappearances of ships and planes in the Bermuda Triangle, a 200,000 square mile area off the Atlantic Coast, with apexes at the Virgin Islands, Bermuda, and a point in the Gulf of Mexico west of Florida.

Edgar Cayce, who received psychic messages while out of his body, said a sunken metropolis exists under the sea in the Triangle near Bimini Island, fifty miles east of Miami. He believed that life originated on a lost continent called Atlantis, supposedly located in that area, and that people today have been reincarnated through many entities into present forms.

Darwin Gross of Menlo Park, California, had an encounter with the parallel world several years ago when another "pair of hands" grabbed the wheel of his car when it was about to crash. He came out of the incident alive and devoted to the one who helped him—Eckankar.

Known as the ancient science of soul travel, the modern Eckankar cult traces its origins to Atlantis.[3]

Psychic Ed Snedeker claims he has contacted an RAF pilot who went down in the Triangle in 1945. "When I searched for him and found him in 1969, he was still alive," Snedeker says. "Know where he was? Somewhere down within the hollow of the Earth!"[4]

M.B. Dykshoorn of Miami, Florida, says a giant whirlpool originating from a hole in the ocean floor in the Triangle is responsible for the strange disappearances of ships and planes.

Seeress Page Bryant draws a similar conclusion, explaining the alleged phenomenon as a tube of energy that extends through the globe from a point in the Triangle to its corresponding sector in the Pacific Ocean south of Japan known as the Devil's Sea, where ships also have disappeared under mysterious circumstances.[5]

Could Dykshoorn's hole be the entrance to a nonphysical parallel world in the subterranean depths? What happens to those who enter the energy tube suggested by Mrs. Bryant?

"They dematerialize and pass on into another dimension," she asserts. "They're dead to us on this plane, but their energies, their spirits, go on. I know because on the first flight we made over the Triangle, I made transmedium contact with one of the gunners who disappeared December 5, 1945.[6] His name is Robert Francis Gallivan, and during one of the hypnosis sessions, he told me: " 'My God, let me tell what's happened!' "[7]

The Bible has similarities and correlations to these theories.

Bryant, Snedeker and Cayce say they have contacted departed spirits in the area of the Triangle. The biblical Hell is described as a place of departed spirits and said to be a parallel world located under the sea.[8]

Eckankar claims it originated in Atlantis. The Bible refers to disembodied spirits, which possibly had their release at the fall of Lucifer and the subsequent destruction of Earth. Are these spirits the entities encountered by soul-hoppers in the next dimension? Could one of them have been Gross' mysterious "pair of hands?"

Dykshoorn sees a hole in the Earth. One of the meanings of the Bible's Hades is literally a subterranean pit or hole. The Bible includes a nether world in these prophetical words: "Wherefore God also hath highly exalted him [Christ], and given him a name which is above every name: that at the name of Jesus every knee should bow, of things in heaven, and things in earth, and things under the earth."[9]

Could the nether regions described by the Bible and psychics be the same?

Another theory is offered by Jacques Bergier, a French scientist who suggests secret passageways lead to seven other worlds within the visible Earth, which he calls energy levels or dwipas.

On one dwipa "lives the King of the World, who safeguards that which is essential to humanity, its spiritual aspirations," he contends. "It is possible to go to the city of the King of the World and come back. It is also possible to encounter on Earth its messengers just returning. And lastly, it is possible to receive a teaching that originates from this city."[10]

While not supporting his theory, the Bible does provide some interesting parallels. Satan, for example, is called the "god of this world," [11] and the Bible describes his influence on human spiritual aspirations. The idea of travel to and from the spiritual and physical realms also is supported by the Bible.

Demonic beings could account for Bergier's dwipa messengers, and the fact that teachings from the spirit world have invaded the religious philosophies of today is evident in occult teachings, and is predicted by the Bible.

Bergier's belief that the frontier between Earth and the invisible parallel worlds can be easily crossed could account for the apparent ease with which many occultists can project into astral planes.

Robert Monroe theorizes that all of the aspects we attribute to Heaven and Hell lie in the plane he calls Locale II. By Earth's standards, he reports, time is nonexistent in this locale. While one senses a sequence of events, a past and a future, there is no cyclical separation. Both coexist as "now."[12]

Could this explain how John, while in exile on the island of Patmos, viewed centuries ago an event planned for our distant future, which appeared to be happening in his present? The incident is recorded this way in Revelation 21:1-3:

> And I saw a new heaven and a new earth:
> for the first heaven and the first earth were
> passed away; and there was no more sea.
>
> And I John saw the holy city, new
> Jerusalem, coming down from God out of
> heaven, prepared as a bride adorned for
> her husband.
>
> And I heard a great voice out of heaven
> saying, Behold, the tabernacle of God is
> with men. . . .

Locale II, to which Monroe says he has traveled many times, "is a state of being where that which we label thought is the wellspring of existence. It is the vital, creative force that produces energy, assembles 'matter' into form, and provides channels of perception and communication. As you think, so you are," he asserts.

"In this environment, no mechanical supplements are found. No cars, boats, airplanes, or rockets are needed for transportation. You think movement, and it is fact. No telephones, radio, television and other communication aids have value. Communication is instantaneous. Mere thought is the force that supplies any need or desire. . . . Like attracts like. Your destination seems to be grounded completely within the framework of your innermost constant motivations, emotions and desires. You may not consciously want to 'go' there, but you have no choice."[13]

Characteristics of this locale are found in the out-of-the-body experiences of the dying. Again, a parallel is evident between Monroe's observations and biblical truth. Those whose emotions and desires were motivated by evil in this life are destined to the abyss, while individuals with a righteous nature ascend to Heaven.

Monroe believes Locale II is the natural environment of the second body, explaining why most of his experiments in astral travel took him "somewhere" onto that plane.

Locale II has no specific location, but is a vast realm consisting of perhaps many dimensions coexisting with the physical planes of the universe. According to Monroe, Locale II "seems to interpenetrate our physical world, yet spans limitless reaches beyond comprehension." He argues the existence of "an infinity of worlds all operative at different frequencies, one of which is this physical world."[14] "Where," in his theory, is "here." Assuming an infinite number of spirit-world possibilities, many planes may inhabit Locale II. Could Heaven and Hell be two of them?

Realms of Illusion

Michael Brod makes a biblically sound observation about one astral dimension, which he terms the "soulish" realm. "This parallel world, where supernatural phenomena which are not of God can be manifested, is the realm spoken of by occultists and sorcerers. I believe that it also is the 'air' over which Satan rules as the 'god of this world.'

"The 'air' is the plane to which a willful astral projector travels. Though connected to the physical world, this realm is distinctly different, vastly expanded, and much more immediate and fluidic in its experiences and impressions."

Brod sees this world as an arena of deception, for it is the occult concept that once one's own awareness has departed from its usual confines of sensory perception, one has entered the true realm of the Holy Spirit.

"This is far from the truth," Brod argues. "It is evident that Satan can cause deception by duplicating the workings of God." This dimension of the other side is a distinct world of illusion, where Satan has the power to imitate the true realms of the Spirit.

Though from an occult point of view, Monroe also brings insight to this concept. What appears to be solid matter and artifacts common to the physical world in Locale II comes from three sources, he notes.

First, they are the *products of thoughts* by those who once lived in the space-time world.

Second, departed souls who liked certain material things in the earthly life have *recreated* them to enhance their surroundings.

Third, beings of a higher order of intelligence *simulate* the physical environment—temporarily at least—for the benefit of those just emerging from the physical world after death.[15]

Could Monroe be right? If like attracts like, could many of those destined to return have traveled to the plane of illusion because they were not spiritually prepared for the ultimate realm of the beyond? Have these people come back with false impressions of the other side, deceived into thinking they are ready for eternity?

Numerous out-of-the-body experiences suggest that Monroe's observations in Locale II are more than theory.

Dorothy Whippo of Terre Haute, Indiana, left her body in May 1939 during a serious illness and visited the astral plane. She tells her experience this way:

I was in a room where four of my closest relatives sat around a table—my father, my brother, his wife, and my favorite uncle. All of them were deceased. But now I saw them again, and they motioned me to join them in a fifth, empty chair.

I was not shocked, nor afraid, for I was aware I had left my body in my sickbed at home. I had been terribly ill with typhoid fever. As my spirit left my body, I found myself moving down a dark corridor toward a light in a doorway. When I went through the doorway, there sat my deceased relatives, in a huge room, bare except for the table and chairs.

My father spoke to me. He had always called me "Sis." Now he said: "Won't you please sit down with us, Sis?" He smiled as he spoke, and the others smiled, too. I felt joyous—it was so wonderful to be with them again!

But something—I don't know what —kept me from sitting down. . . .[16]

Woody Thornton of Birmingham, Alabama, suffered a severe heart attack on May 6, 1972, and was rushed to Veterans Administration Hospital. His heart stopped beating, and while doctors worked to revive him, Thornton says, his spirit traveled to the other side. He recalls the incident:

The next I knew, I was knocking on a tall, wooden door like that of an old cathedral. It swung open to reveal an old man with a white beard who was wearing a white robe. I'd always heard St. Peter stands guard at the gates of Heaven. So I said, "St. Peter?"

He nodded and asked who I was and what I wanted. "My name is Woody Thornton," I said, "and I want to come in."

The saint left for a moment. I looked around and realized there was nothing there but me, the door and clouds. I was just floating in space. St. Peter returned carrying a huge, old book. He opened it, looked inside, and said my name wasn't listed. He told me to go back to mortal life.

All of a sudden, I came to back in the hospital. I could see the doctors and nurses sighing with relief at the return of my life.[17]

Andrew Kosh of Avenel, New Jersey, tells a fascinating tale of a strange journey he took while on the verge of death. His cardiac arrest was confirmed by Dr. Milton Bronstein of Edison, New Jersey. Here is Kosh's account:

There I was—somewhere between Heaven and Hell—and rejected by both. I was about to panic when a voice sounded out sharp and clear: "It is not your time!"

In my unconscious state, I found myself running down a long road. It suddenly divided, one fork leading down a long hill and the other up the hill. I decided to take the one going down. I had always felt I would wind up in Hell anyway.

After what seemed like an endless journey downward, I saw a great many people—all without faces—milling about in a packed arena. Then several voices called out to me: "You don't belong here!"

Without hesitation, I went racing back up the hill. It was a long, tiring struggle, but when I reached the top I could see the gates of Heaven, wide open.

But as I drew nearer, two gatekeepers began to close the gates. They were completely closed when I reached them. Then came that powerful voice, uttering words I'll never forget: "It is not your time!" I was so relieved, I seemed to gain added strength and started back down the road.[18]

Why do spirit-world beings simulate a physical environment for those just entering the beyond? Their purpose, Monroe suggests, is to reduce trauma and shock for the "newcomers" by introducing familiar shapes and settings in the early conversion stages.

While I do not agree with this conclusion, Monroe's simulation theory is significant. So much of the world's occult literature speaks of "another world" that is similar to biblical and Christian out-of-the-body descriptions of heavenly places.

Typical are the experiences of a Los Angeles man and a ten-year-old boy.

James Larson suffered a heart attack and died, spending five minutes in the beyond before the physician in charge, Dr. Samuel Weisman, brought him back.

"I felt myself floating in the air and could clearly see my body lying down there," Lorne recalls. "I landed in a long corridor filled with soft twilight. At the end a bright light was shining. I could also hear voices coming from there.

"When I reached the end of the tunnel or corridor, I came out into a splendid garden with trees bearing all kinds of fruit. Stretching out, too, before my eyes were meadows with bright flowers in bloom. Everywhere people were standing about in groups, conversing. But when I began to move closer, the scene always receded in front of me. Nobody seemed to be aware of my shouts, my desire to stay there."[19]

Ten-year-old Otto Borgnein was crushed under a wall when it collapsed, and he lay in the hospital for days in a deep coma. Dr. Peter Klein, who took care of him, said that "twice during those five days the boy was clinically dead." Here is what Hans related to the doctor after he recovered:

> I felt wonderful. Twice I visited another country. There were a lot of children there playing outdoors and in big, golden cities. I wanted to play with them, but they told me I wouldn't have time.
>
> The first time I went away I saw children outdoors, with such wonderful toys I didn't want ever to go away. They had instruments which they made nice music with and flowers that you could see growing.
>
> The second time I saw a great big city made of solid gold and filled with kids. They were so happy. We laughed together. When everything disappeared all of a sudden, I was awfully sad because I knew I had to come back here."[20]

Many of those who momentarily travel beyond their immediate death scene often go to tranquil realms closely resembling the blissful splendors of Heaven, yet their encounters are void of spiritual meaning and riddled with moral indifference. Could these realms be simulations? Many illusions await the unprepared who venture beyond.

Turning Light on Satan

As I have said, an experience common among those who exit their bodies is the encounter with the being of light whose personality emanates indescribable love and warmth. The identity attributed to this incredible being, Raymond Moody learned, varies with the religious background of the individual. To a Christian, it is Christ. To a Jew, an angel. To one without religious training, just a being of light.[21]

Who is this light? Jesus said, "I am the light of the world."[22] The Bible says, "God is light, and in him is no darkness at all."[23] Angels are depicted in the Bible as light beings.[24] But there is another entity out there who is the master of disguise—and one of his costumes is light. The Bible identifies him as "Satan himself . . . transformed into an angel of light."[25]

Before his fall, Satan was a light being whose aura was dazzling.[26] His angelic name, Lucifer, literally means light-bearer. Angels lighted the hillsides when they came to announce the birth of Christ.[27] It would not be too surprising then if their counterparts—fallen angels—could appear as light, too.

Moody makes a serious mistake in dealing with this issue. Because the being of light always speaks good things and envelops his subjects with warmth and compassion, he assumes it must be benevolent. He concludes:

It seems to me that the best way of distinguishing between God-directed and Satan-directed experiences would be to see what the person involved does and says after his experience. God, I suppose, would try to get those to whom he appears to be loving and forgiving. Satan would presumably tell his servants to follow a course of hate and destruction.

Manifestly, my subjects have come back with a renewed commitment to follow the former course and to disavow the latter. In the light of all the machinations which a hypothetical demon would have to have carried out in order to delude his hapless victim (and to what purpose?), he certainly has failed miserably—as far as I can tell—to make persuasive emissaries for his program![28]

While it is true that what a person does and says after his experience can indicate a God-directed or Satan-directed experience, to conclude that Satan would urge a course of hate and destruction to a soul visiting the other side is to ignore the devil's character—and purpose. If you had an out-of-the-body experience and met a being of light who said it's okay to lie, cheat, murder, and steal, would you be delighted or disgusted? Too much evidence in the Bible and in everyday life of this light-bearer's deception and motives is available to consider seriously Moody's theory.

Because most who encounter the being of light return as more loving individuals, some find it hard to accept the possibility that theirs was an encounter with Satan. But Lucifer once experienced the purity of God's love, and as an angelic being could be loving. The memory of this, and the pain of his loss, tortures him. Driven by fierce hate, this bionic rebel of the universe imitates love to destroy those whom he deceives, and with vengeful skill.

We can expect little else from Lucifer than that he would appear as a righteous being, advocating love and forgiveness in order to sidetrack people into immoral lives.

If Satan can delude people on Earth into rationalizing even the greatest sins, how much more can he fool someone entering his own realm, where humanity—the child of the universe—is totally ignorant and gullible?

Of course, the being of light is not always Lucifer. Many have met Jesus as the being of light with life-transforming results. But one needs to judge encounters by applying the tests listed earlier to make sure that the entity is the Lord.

Deception is revealed in the experiences of Michael and Mary-Ann Brod, who journeyed deep into the occult in their search for God. The Brods began to communicate with spirits who appeared as lights, claiming to be of God. Many times these spirits left them feeling spiritually high. Here's how she recalls their experiences:

> These spirits said they were of God and that man was disconnected from God. They said they would reconnect us with God.
>
> Because we wanted Him, we were gullible. The spirits told us good things about God. They told us good ways to lead our lives. They promised to open up the past so we can really be in fellowship with

God. Because they said they were from God, we reasoned, how could they not be? . . . We couldn't even consider the fact that they might actually be evil. But by the time we found they were evil, supernatural things were happening in our lives.

It was possible for our conscious minds to leave our bodies and to actually travel in what is termed the astral world. I know now that those "higher planes" is the space Satan occupies (Ephesians 2:2).

My husband was able to know what people were thinking; he was able to lay his hands on people and give an appearance of healing. We have since discovered that when one is in harmony with Satan, he can take the symptoms off a person so they believe they are healed. In this way, the person has believed a false doctrine.

I'd been looking for God for nine years. My husband had been looking for 18 years. I kept having the overwhelming sense that what we were involved in was really evil. When Michael and I talked, I realized that I was looking at my husband with new eyes. I saw the way he was, and I said, "No, this is evil." And when I could see that it was evil, it was like my whole world collapsed.[29]

Realizing this, an intense inner struggle for the truth began, ending when she committed her life to Christ at Massapequa Tabernacle in New York. Her husband was converted and delivered of demon possession soon afterward. She looks back on her life with these comments:

I did not really understand what I was doing. I did it trying to have a good heart. But I just got totally misled.

We're going to walk with Jesus. When Satan comes against us with any kind of unbelief—no matter what it is, if it's not in the Word of God—I will not accept it in my life.

No Fear of Dying

Losing the fear of death is an experience shared by many who depart the body and return. Typical is the case of the famous comedian Jack Benny, described as one who had a violent fear of death. Witnessing a beautiful life beyond the grave, Benny whispered to his aide, Eddie Villery, "I just saw Lyman Woods and spoke to him. He is going to help me through. He showed me the way . . . and it is beautiful." It was evident Benny no longer feared death, Villery observes.

Woods, who had been Benny's vaudeville partner, had been dead for forty-five years. Shortly before his own death, Benny told Villery:

I was with Lyman. He told me it was beautiful—and it was . . . it was![30]

Hazel Freeman of California also says she no longer fears death since her out-of-the-body trip:

I remember I was standing on the grassy bank of a wide river. The sun was shining. My father, who had died many years before when I was 10, was standing on the far bank, waving to me and calling for me to cross over.

Suddenly, the whole scene vanished, and I was back in my hospital room, floating strangely above my own bed. I could see my body down below. My spirit had left my body. . . .

Since then I have had no fear of death or life hereafter. I am sure I glimpsed both in that hospital room 22 years ago.[31]

Are malevolent beings creating these illusions so that many who visit the beyond will return to anesthetize a gullible world to the terrifying realities of judgment awaiting the unprepared?

We cannot discern the destiny of anyone who returns no longer afraid to die, for Christians and non-Christians alike share this change. But unless one has established a personal relationship with Christ, the loss of fear could be rooted in deception.

In Hazel Freeman's account, a glaring clue to deception is apparent. In the world she visited, the sun was shining. But the Bible says, "There shall be no night there; and they need no candle, neither light of the sun; for the Lord God giveth them light. . . ."[32] Whatever realm she saw, it was not Heaven.

In Hebrews 2:14 Jesus is described as the destroyer of him who has the power of death—Satan. How cunning it is of this being of light to counterfeit even the work of Christ in ridding us of the fear of death by circumventing the cross! If no judgment awaits the non-Christian, only a welcoming by the light-being into endless bliss, the death of Jesus Christ would be meaningless. Often, departed spirits travel through a "dark tunnel" to this light. What an opportunity for Satan to don his garments of light and play the hero at the end of the tunnel!

No Hell?

Moody acknowledges that, in most cases he studied, the concepts of reward and punishment in the afterlife are abandoned or disavowed, even by those who once believed in such. He observes:

> They found, much to their amazement, that even when their most apparently awful and sinful deeds were made manifest before the being of light, the being responded not with anger and rage, but rather only with understanding, and even humor.
>
> Through all of my research . . . I have not heard a single reference to a heaven or a hell anything like the customary picture to which we are exposed in this society. Indeed, many persons have stressed how unlike their experiences were to what they had been led to expect in the course of their religious training.
>
> One woman who "died" reported: "I had always heard that when you die, you see both Heaven and Hell, but I didn't see either one."[33]

David Wheeler, another investigator of out-of-the-body phenomena, has a different observation. While most of those he interviewed had happy experiences, "some returned filled with horror and displeasure. Some thought that they had visited Hell and had been lucky enough to be brought back to this life. Some did not have a good recollection of their time while dead, yet something affected their subconscious minds negatively, and it has stayed with them."[34]

Dr. Maurice Rawlins, a cardiologist and one-time personal physician to three United States generals, including Dwight D. Eisenhower, tells of a patient who had a horrifying experience.

One day a man came into the hospital for a checkup, complaining of chest pains. After a few moments on the treadmill, the patient said to the attending nurse, "You'd better help me. I think I'm about to die."

At first the nurse thought he was joking. But as she giggled, he died. Frightened, she summoned Dr. Rawlins, who was just outside the room, and he worked feverishly to revive the man. Suddenly the dead man screamed, "Don't stop!" Usually patients yell, "You're hurting me!" and beg him to stop, Dr. Rawlins says: But this man wanted desperately to come back.

"Why don't you want me to stop?" Dr. Rawlins quizzed, pounding the man's chest.

"I'm in Hell!" he screamed.

"You mean you're scared of going to Hell."

"I am not. I'm *in* Hell. Don't let me go!"

As he looked at his patient closely for the first time, Dr. Rawlins realized he had not seen such terror on a man's face in twenty-five years.

"How do I stop being in Hell?" the man screamed.

"I'm not a preacher," Dr. Rawlins grunted, continuing his frantic efforts to save the man.

"Please tell me how to stop being in Hell!"

"I'd guess you'd pray a Sunday school prayer," the doctor answered. "Like this, 'Lord Jesus, forgive my sins. Come and live in me. If you spare my life, I'll be hooked on you. If you take my life, take me to Heaven.'"

With that the man died again. Six times Dr. Rawlins brought him back before succeeding in keeping him alive. The physician says people restored to life usually lose total recall of any unpleasant incident at the time of death. This proved true again the next day when he went to see the man with pencil and paper to document his experience.

"Hell? What do you mean, 'Hell'? I wasn't in Hell!" the patient exclaimed.

"That's where you said you were," Dr. Rawlins insisted. "Don't you remember you prayed a prayer with me?"

"I do remember the prayer. I don't remember being in Hell."

Some who came back from the beyond *did* see Hell and remember their experience.

George Godkin of Alberta, Canada, is one of the few who went there and back. He gives this frightening account:

> I was guided to the place in the spirit world called Hell. This is a place of punishment for all those who reject Jesus Christ. I not only saw Hell, but felt the torment that all who go there will experience.

> The darkness of Hell is so intense that it seems to have a pressure per square inch. It is an extremely black, dismal, desolate, heavy, pressurized type of darkness. It gives the individual a crushing, despondent feeling of loneliness.

> The heat is a dry, dehydrating type. Your eyeballs are so dry they feel like red hot coals in their sockets. Your tongue and

lips are parched and cracked with the
intense heat. The breath from your nostrils
as well as the air you breathe feels like a
blast from a furnace. The exterior of your
body feels as though it were encased within
a white hot stove. The interior of your body
has a sensation of scorching hot air being
forced through it.

The agony and loneliness of Hell cannot
be expressed clearly enough for proper
understanding to the human soul; it has to
be experienced.[35]

Unfortunately, the soul bound for Hell cannot
return with a warning if it's the individual's date
with destiny—the reason so few descriptions of this
realm are available.

Another vivid account is related by German actor
Curt Jurgens. He had come to Houston, Texas, to
consult with the famed Dr. Michael E. DeBakey
about a severe heart ailment. Dr. DeBakey advised
the actor to have his aorta replaced with a plastic
artery, a grave surgical risk. Although told his
chances to survive were only fifty percent and that
his heart would be stopped for a few minutes during
the procedure, Jurgens decided to have the
four-hour operation. Here are excerpts from his
account:

Soon I had a feeling that life was ebbing
from me. I felt powerful sensations of
dread. I had been looking up into the big
glass cupola over the operating room. This
cupola now began to change. Suddenly it
turned a glowing red. I saw twisted faces
grimacing as they stared down at me.

I tried to struggle upright and defend myself against these ghosts, who were moving closer to me. Then it seemed as if the glass cupola had turned into a transparent dome that was slowly sinking down over me. A fiery rain was now falling, but though the drops were enormous, none of them touched me. They splattered down around me, and out of them grew menacing tongues of flames licking up about me.

I could no longer shut out the frightful truth: beyond doubt, the faces dominating this fiery world were faces of the damned. I had a feeling of despair. . . the sensation of horror was so great it choked me.

Obviously I was in Hell itself, and the glowing tongues of fire could be reaching me any minute. In this situation, the black silhouette of a human figure suddenly materialized and began to draw near. It was a woman in a black veil, a slender woman with a lipless mouth and in her eyes an expression that sent icy shudders down my back.

She stretched out her arms toward me and, pulled by an irresistible force, I followed her. An icy breath touched me, and I came into a world filled with faint sounds of lamentation, though there was not a person in sight. Then and there I asked the figure to tell me who she was. A voice answered: "I am death."

I summoned all my strength and thought: "I'll not follow her any more, for I want to live."[36]

A battle ensued between Jurgens and the veiled figure until he finally broke loose from her magnetic spell and felt the severe, dull pain in his chest signaling his return to life.

Those who declare Hell doesn't exist because they haven't seen it, as in Moody's examples, have inadvertently become part of the deception—a lie that is fortified by illusions of peace and beauty granted those spirits who naively venture into the beyond. It is Satan's scheme to entertain unsuspecting souls with experiences similar to those reserved for spiritually reborn Christians, for in the process he can lull humanity into thinking it doesn't need a Savior.

Weird World of Locale III

Is Monroe's Locale II the only illusory plane in the beyond? During a series of astral experiments, the psychic visited what he calls Locale III. To summarize his observations, this plane appears to be a physical matter world almost identical to our own. "The natural environment is the same," he notes. "There are homes, families, businesses, and people work for a living. There are roads on which vehicles travel. There are railroads and trains."[37]

Although Locale III seems nearly like Earth, it is not identical, he notes. Carefully studying his environment during out-of-the-body trips there, he concludes the locale is not some part of our world unknown to him.

Despite the similarities between Locale III and Earth, too many differences are apparent, he argues. Scientific development is inconsistent with either our past or present, habits and social customs are unlike ours, and history is different. Often in this realm, Monroe occupied the body of a man, temporarily living his life and puzzling his friends by suspicious behavior.[38]

During his excursions, did Monroe discover life on another planet? Did he visit a world very much like our own, yet unique in its orbit around another sun? As we have seen in chapter 4, astral projectors have demonstrated their ability to travel to other planets in our solar system. Another possibility exists that Locale III could be an astral plane of a higher order. If so, perhaps spirit entities imitated the physical dimension so well that Monroe became a victim of their amusement.

Fifth Dimension Adventure

Anything can happen in the fifth dimension[39] where other-world entities are free to roam and victimize those who temporarily venture into their territory.

Here is an illustration from Monroe's own experience:

> On one non-physical excursion, I was speeding through nothing back to the physical with everything apparently well under control. Without warning, I rammed into a solid wall of some impenetrable material. I wasn't hurt, but I was utterly shocked.
>
> The material was hard and solid, and seemed to be made of huge plates of steel overlapping slightly and welded together. Each had a slight curvature as if part of a globe.
>
> I tried to push through it, but could not. I went up, down, to the right, and to the left. I was absolutely sure my physical body lay

beyond this barrier.

After what seemed an hour of scratching, clawing and pushing at this barrier, I prayed. I used every prayer I had ever learned, and made up a few special ones. And I meant every word more than I had ever meant anything in my life. I was that frightened.

Nothing happened. I was still plastered against the barrier, unable to get through and back to my physical body.

I panicked. I clawed, screamed and sobbed. After this proved futile, I finally calmed down only out of emotional exhaustion. Feeling lost, I lay there and rested, clinging to the cold, hard wall.[40]

The astral planes of the occult could be where evil spirits dwell, commuting about the universe until their final expulsion and punishment.[41] If so, it is easy to understand why many people have encountered malevolent beings during astral excursions and why illusions abound in the beyond.

Although out-of-the-body experiences reported by Christians and non-Christians may seem similar, a significant difference exists.

A personal relationship with Christ prepares us for Heaven, guaranteeing a direct flight, should the out-of-the-body episode last long enough for us to depart our corporeal home. The tests mentioned in chapter 2 provide solid clues to the nature of one's experience so that we would not be deceived by a look-alike destination.

The difference also is evident in the glimpses of heavenly realities reported by people who have committed their lives to Christ.

6

Encounters of the Heavenly Kind

The peaceful spring morning was shattered by the screeching howl of tires as a speeding driver tried to control his car.

"It sounds like somebody's going to be hit!" cried former Assistant Secretary of the Navy James E. "Johnny" Johnson to his passenger. Dr. Johnson was waiting for a traffic light en route to a business appointment outside Washington, D.C.

In a split second the screams of crushing metal drowned the last of Johnson's words as a big Mercury plowed at high speed into the rear of his car. His head snapped back; his body was hurled into the steering column. A stabbing pain shot from his shoulder as it rammed the wheel, while his head and right arm continued through, wedging him tightly against the dash. Everything went dark.

In a moment he felt himself floating gently in the darkness toward a suddenly bright light. It was as if he had been traveling a dark country road and had just popped over a hilltop to be dazzled by a brilliant sunrise. The feeling was exquisitely beautiful.

Intuitively he knew that the brilliance was Christ.

99

Enchanted by a sense of peace and delightful lightness, Johnson turned his gaze below to the scene of the accident. Without the slightest desire to return, he felt strangely unconcerned with the lifeless body tangled in that wreckage.

"Don't move that guy!" shouted an ambulance attendant. "Bet his neck is broken."

Attorney Jack Snyder, the car's passenger, was pacing about the wreck, trying to help the rescuers. "What can I do?" he begged.

"Just stand back. We'll do it!" an attendant snapped.

Johnny Johnson observed the accident scene from the beyond, watching police control spectators and interview witnesses, while firemen and ambulance attendants frantically pried at the mangled car to pull his limp body out of the wreckage.

Soon he saw his wife, Juanita, standing there, smiling at him. She had never looked more beautiful. Her face seemed alive with happiness. Puzzled, he wondered if she had come in spirit to wish him well on his journey to Heaven.

Meanwhile, Juanita, sitting at home that morning, had sensed the moment that the accident had occurred. Having a vision of the scene, she knew that her husband had left the Earth. She began to pray fervently that God would bring him back to life, receiving assurance that her prayer would be answered. When the police knocked on her door with news of the accident, she was not surprised.

Reassured by the beautiful vision of his wife, Johnson lost interest in the accident scene. With eyes turned heavenward in anticipation, all became dark again. He describes his journey:

I flew headlong through a dark tunnel at

accelerating speed toward the shimmering light I sensed was Christ. As I approached its radiant beauty, I was bathed in indescribable love.

Inside this light was a celestial city, like a castle in the sky. The translucent golden streets glowed with the brilliance that illuminated the whole city. I had the sense of being in and with this light of Christ. An incredible feeling of freedom and peace filled me with a sense of absolute beauty. I knew I was in Heaven.

Soon I saw Ken, my son who had been called to Heaven years before. He was dressed in dazzling white, reminding me of the gown he had worn when he was baptized. His face beamed with the same love he had shown on that day. "Take care of Mommy and the children," Ken smiled.

Suddenly, I felt a tug as though someone were trying to draw me back to Earth. I sensed Juanita was praying that I would return to her. I began to feel heavy as the pull of her prayer persisted, but I did not want to go back to that pain-wracked body. Heaven was too beautiful to leave.

Then I recognized my father-in-law, with his special way of smiling and that little squint in his eyes I had known so well. "You'll be all right," he said. "Go on back. Go on back. Go on back."

Others around him picked up the chant. "Go on back. Go on back," they sang, and I knew I had to return.

My own mother and father joined the chant. My mother pointed to the light and asked, "Did you see Him?" I answered, "Yes," with deep reverence. Caught up in the pervasive love and total peace of that place, I could not imagine leaving. Yet, I knew I must. My time had not come.

The accident scene came into focus again. Suddenly, I felt very heavy, as if someone had laid an iron weight on top of me. As I began floating toward my body, a growing sensation of pain filled my consciousness.

The shimmering light of heavenly love slowly dissolved into a harsh, flashing red light. I was back in my body, and the rescue squad was still trying to pull me out of the steering wheel.

After his supernatural experience, Johnson refused to be encased in a broken body. In the ambulance his prayer took on a new dimension of faith as he asked God for complete healing that day. With an other-world perception, he knew it would happen.

The ambulance attendants and the doctors only laughed when their patient announced he would walk home that day fully recovered. He was considered delirious.

X-rays at the hospital revealed a hairline fracture of the neck. The right arm and leg were paralyzed and completely numb, indicating brain damage. The prognosis was a long hospital stay and twelve to eighteen months of intensive physical therapy.

Yet, with his newly deepened faith, Johnson withstood the ridicule, insisting he would walk out of the hospital that day a whole man. To the amazement of attending medical personnel, he was able to move his arm and leg immediately after the

X-rays were taken. The pain suddenly subsided, and after further examination, the baffled doctors released him. By the time he arrived home, he wasn't even sore!

As a result of this miraculous incident, an ambulance attendant and one doctor made decisions for Christ before he left the hospital.

Johnny Johnson's story* is a thrilling example of how godly encounters in the afterworld have life-changing results in this world.

Life into Eternal Life

For John and Denise Beck, the day after Christmas 1976 held tragedy. While enjoying the clear, blue skies in their two-seater airplane, the craft was jarred by a loud pop in the engine compartment. Without power, John desperately attempted an emergency landing near Lake Elsinore, California.

As the ground rushed toward them, John pulled back on the controls with all his strength. "Hang on! Brace yourself!" he yelled seconds before the plane hit nose wheel first on the plowed field and bounced high into the air. John and Denise were hurled hard against the instrument panel. Within seconds both of them lost consciousness.

John died from a massive brain hemorrhage. Denise suddenly felt herself in extreme darkness, accompanied by a roaring, buzzing sound. Suddenly, a pure white light filled her consciousness, flooding her with a tremendous feeling of love and peace.

Gazing into the light, she saw Jesus facing her,

---

* For the full biography of James E. "Johnny" Johnson, read *Beyond Defeat* as told to David Balsiger (Doubleday, New York, 1978).

dressed in a blue transparent robe over a light blue gown. Standing by Jesus' side was her husband, flashing an overwhelmingly beautiful smile of happiness and love. Strangely, he was not dressed in his flying clothes, but in a blue grey three-piece suit—the very suit, Denise later learned, in which he was buried.

Seeing John so happy, Denise wanted to join him and stay there forever. But Jesus told her to return to Earth and to her baby son.

"It will be hard," Jesus said comfortingly, "but do not worry. John will be happy with me here for eternity. Give all your love to God, and tell others that there is life into eternal life after death."

Jesus explained to her the parts of the Bible she had found puzzling, and they immediately became clear. Determined to serve Christ with all her heart, she promised: "I'll do anything you ask, Lord."

As Jesus put His robe around John, Denise was suddenly plunged back into darkness, reentering her body lying death-like in the airplane wreckage.

"Help me!" she called weakly as a man bent over her, nearly scaring him out of his wits.

Later in the hospital—her neck and skull fractured, and arm broken—the doctors were amazed by her joy and rapid recovery.

"I would have lost my mind in the hospital had it not been for what I had seen and for what Jesus told me," Denise says.

"I'm not afraid of dying now, though I was then. It's nothing to be afraid of. And I have a clearer understanding of God's Word. It's overwhelming! Often when I read the Bible, I realize, 'Hey! That's just what Jesus said!' "[1]

A Spirit Being Said, "Come"

About 1:30 P.M. on January 7, 1948, George Godkin's home was rocked by a gas explosion. Caught in the basement during the ensuing fire, his only alternative was to escape through the searing flames in the kitchen.

Suffering from third-degree burns over sixty-five percent of his body, his ears burned off and nose gone to the bone, Godkin was rushed to the hospital by a neighbor. During the critical days ahead, he had a strange spiritual experience.

"When the room was empty of doctors and nurses, I became aware of a presence in my room standing near the foot of the bed," he recalls. "Then I saw a square of light like a small window on the wall near the ceiling. While lying there swathed in bandages from head to foot admiring this beautiful light, I watched it become larger and larger, finally filling the entire area beside my bed. Half the room was normal light, while the other was of this supernatural quality. I could see a distinct difference between the two areas."

Godkin noticed that the spiritual being at the foot of his bed was now inside the light. "I was made to understand that He was responsible for its existence. This presence appeared to be so pure and holy that I suddenly became conscious of being vile and sinful by comparison. I became so convinced of my sinful condition that I began confessing my sins one by one to the spiritual person who was in the light. At the precise moment of complete surrender, several things happened in quick succession. I noticed that my right arm was stretched out toward the light. As I yielded myself completely, someone dressed in white walked past me, and the hem of His garment penetrated to the second knuckle of my right hand. Suddenly, the tremendous weight of sin lifted, and I had a wonderful feeling of cleanness and purity inside."

A short time later another spirit being entered the room and said, "Come." At the angel's command, Godkin left his body. After a quick look at his breathing physical form lying on the bed, Godkin suddenly found himself in a paradise world.

"I saw that the light radiated from Jesus Christ, the Son of the living God," he recalls. "No words can express the softness, gentleness, and life-giving virtue that this light contains. It fills the entire area in Heaven called Paradise. I do not know the size of this plane, but when I looked in every direction I could see no end. Each one of us who has caught glimpses of the spiritual world is only allowed to view what God wants him to see.

"Although different beings and things exist in the spiritual world which I was not privileged to see, volumes would be needed to contain in detail all that I did see and hear."

Assuming he was there to stay, Godkin was shocked and disappointed when it came time for his return. "So I begged and pleaded for permission to remain," he says, "but I was told to return and tell what I saw."

"I Rode in a Heavenly Vehicle"

Rev. R.A. Work, the late father-in-law of Dr. Ralph Wilkerson, pastor of Melodyland Christian Center in Anaheim, California, died in March 1938 from injuries suffered in a fall of nearly two stories onto a concrete basement floor.

Shortly after he came back to life in answer to prayer, he related this account:

I was with the Lord. I rode in a heavenly

vehicle through space toward a bright light. The light got brighter and brighter as the craft got closer. I stopped at the gate to a magnificent city with a beauty indescribable.

I was surrounded by angels and loved ones and could see inside the city. I saw streets of gold and other splendors I have no words to describe. I could see people who had passed on to be with the Lord.

Just as I was about to be ushered through the pearly gates, two heavenly beings stopped me. "You can't go through," they said. "You must return. Your work is not finished."

"But why do I have to go back?" I pleaded. One of the angels said, "There's a prayer that must be answered. You have to go back."

Twenty-two years later in 1960 Rev. Work was pastoring a different congregation. Coming home one day with the symptoms of a heart attack, he went to his bedroom and sat on the edge of the bed. His wife called an ambulance and began praying, hoping to keep him alive with her prayers as she had done years ago. But before the ambulance arrived, he was gone. God had extended his life until their children were married and his work was finished.[2]

"I Was in a Holy Place"
Margaret Bell of Miami, Florida, returned from Heaven with a mission similar to Godkin's. Suffering from acute congestive heart failure following abdominal surgery, Mrs. Bell suddenly felt herself soaring through the twilight of space until she came

to a gigantic, beautiful wall. To her amazement, she floated right through it.

"When I came out on the other side, I folded my hands in prayer, for I knew I was in a holy place—Heaven. Everything was bathed in a soft, golden light," she relates. "I realized this warm, beautiful light came from the Lord because the Bible says: 'I am the Light of the world, and I am the way.'[3]

"I gazed over green valleys, and in the distance I saw enormous mansions of pink and white alabaster. Towering above these houses was a colossal building of dazzling whiteness."

She tried to get closer but was suddenly returned to her body.

"I'm sure my life was spared because the Lord has some missions for me," she affirms. "One of them is to share my beautiful experience in Heaven with others."[4]

"It's Not Your Time"

Betty Baxter of Albuquerque, New Mexico, was born with every vertebrae in her spine out of place. She also suffered from St. Vitus's dance and shook violently from head to toe. Today a picture of health, she was taken on a life-changing journey to witness afterlife realities. Here are excerpts from her account:

> As the years went by, I gave up all hope of getting well through medical care. But I still had faith that God would heal me.
>
> I began to pray to Jesus to come and take me to Heaven. As I prayed, a thick darkness settled over me. I felt coldness creeping through my body. In a moment's

time, I was cold all over and completely surrounded by darkness.

Through the darkness I saw a long, dark, narrow valley. As I went inside this valley, I began to scream. I knew this must be the Valley of Death. I had prayed to die, and to get to Jesus I would have to walk it. I started forward.

I had barely gotten inside when the place lit up with the light of day. I felt something strong and firm take hold of my hand. I didn't need to look. I knew it was the nail-scarred hand of the Son of God who had saved my soul.

He took my hand and held it tightly, and I went on through the valley. I wasn't afraid any more. I was happy, for now I was going home. My mother had said in Heaven I would have a new body, one that would be straight instead of bent and twisted and crippled.

At last we heard music in the distance, the most beautiful music I had ever heard. We quickened our steps. We came to a wide river, separating us from that beautiful land. I looked on the other side and saw green grass, flowers of every color, beautiful flowers that would never die. I saw the river of life wending its way through the city of God. Standing on its banks was a company of those who had been redeemed by the blood of Christ, and they were singing.

At that very moment I heard Jesus say very softly and with great kindness, "No, Betty, it's not your time to cross yet. Go back, for you are going to have healing in the fall."

Instantly I returned to my body and slowly regained consciousness.[5]

I first heard her experience related by Oral Roberts a few years ago in one of his crusades. A few months after she visited the other side, Betty was miraculously healed. The incident occurred in Fairmont, Minnesota, and in bold headlines the *Fairmont Daily Sentinel* carried the story on its front page. Her testimony has inspired thousands to seek a deeper faith in Christ and receive miraculous healings from God.

Could Leave Body at Will

On March 10, 1928, Anna Hewlett Ward made the round trip to Heaven from Birmingham, England. Her testimony solidly proclaims Christ as the source of life and healing.

"When I left my body, I ascended through the air," she related to friends. "As I passed through the first heaven, I could feel the air gently blowing upon my face. Having passed the first heaven, I ascended up through and beyond the stars. I looked down upon the starry realm. What a wonderful sight! I might compare the stars with the lights of a great city as seen from a distance."

Suddenly, she saw the enchanting gold and jasper light of the heavenly city in the distance. Rapidly approaching the radiant, gem-studded metropolis, she was met by an angel who pointed downward, saying, "You must return to Earth again."

Disappointed and anxious to enter the city, Mrs. Ward nevertheless found herself slowly returning to Earth. "My flight to Heaven was rapid. My return to

Earth seemed so slow . . . it was a reluctant return," she lamented. "When I arrived on Earth, I did not at once enter my body, but for a time went back and forth, up and down the street where my body lay, my feet never touching the dirty, earthly street."

When at last in her body, the first word she uttered was "Jesus."

"At every pronouncement of the name, life flowed through my body until all disease and death therein was replaced by life from Him who quickens our mortal bodies," she said.

"As I kept saying 'Jesus,' His divine life flowed into my body until those beside me saw my face radiating a great light brighter than the incandescent light in the room. This was the glory light of the other world that shone on the face of Moses, a light so bright that the children of Israel could not look upon it."[6]

The next day, Mrs. Ward went about her regular duties free from all sickness and disease. Yet, a persistent restlessness haunted her.

"I was restless in the body, having a great longing to return to the heavenly city forever," she reported. "For about ten days I felt that, without any sickness, I could leave my body again at will and fly to the city in the skies."

Carefully and prayerfully guarded by her friends during this period, she soon lost her strange sense of ability to reenter the beyond and was content to remain in her body "until I have finished what He wants me to do here below."[7]

Mixed Emotions

Non-Christians cannot share the testimonies of those who have been spiritually prepared for their journeys beyond. Being vulnerable to deception because of spiritual unpreparedness, the non-Christian receives an unreal image of the other side and is lulled into a false sense of destiny.

Awaiting the Christian who ventures deep into the beyond are the realities of eternity in the presence of God. No illusionary planes are encountered; the flight is direct to Heaven. The experience is transforming.

Indications of non-Christian visits to worlds beyond are apparent in the reactions of many who come back. Some are perplexed over the significance of their journey—as one man said:

> Today, 27 years after it happened, I still don't know the spiritual significance of my experience. I'm a man of science and deal in hard facts—but each time I examine the events of that day, I come up with the same conclusion. [8]

Some are vague. Characteristic responses include a new outlook on life, a better understanding of death and the hereafter, a belief in a second chance beyond the grave, a knowledge that loved ones are waiting in the afterlife, a greater sense of courage and calmness, and no fear of death. Others are comforted in knowing that life doesn't end when one dies, or they are intrigued that forces exist in parallel worlds which are beyond comprehension.

An example of the vagueness of purpose which some relate is revealed by one man's evaluation: "I was saved at the last moment by some Absolute Being after recognizing that I had more to offer life and my fellowman." It is expressed again by a woman who said, "This terrifying brush with death taught me to believe in the existence of a soul which is capable of escaping the body under certain circumstances." And again, "I don't know why I was sent back to Earth."

Misconceptions

Many return with no perceptible change in lives or attitudes. Some come back with misconceptions. One man, for example, became convinced he will return in the next life as another person or another living thing. The futility of this hope lies in the uncertainty of his destiny. Who or what will he become in his reincarnation? A king or a peasant? A scientist or a city councilman? A thief or a rapist? A snake or a cow? A fly or a frog?

While knowledge of the other side brings a measure of comfort to most, the misconceptions spawned in the parallel planes can be tormenting.

Robert Monroe suffered a feeling of utter despair during one excursion to the fifth dimension. There he encountered a "cold intelligence," which he theorized "may be the omnipotence we call God." He describes this moment:

> By this time, it was getting light, and I sat down and cried, great deep sobs as I have never cried before, because then I knew without any qualification or future hope of change that the God of my childhood, of the churches, of religion throughout the world was not as we worshiped him to be—that for the rest of my life, I would suffer the loss of this illusion.[9]

The testimonies of committed Christians are significant by contrast.

Revolutionized Lives

Betty Baxter inspired faith in thousands of people, leading them to a life in Christ.

Anna Ward claimed Christ as the source of her life and healing.

Margaret Bell and George Godkin returned with a sense of mission to share their experiences so others would know the realities and rewards waiting in Heaven.

Johnny Johnson came back with deepened faith for the miraculous, resulting not only in his own incredible physical recovery, but in the conversion of a doctor and an ambulance attendant.

Denise Beck returned with a clearer understanding of the Bible, vowing to tell others that Christian death is a "life into eternal life" experience.

Some are thanking and praising God for their miraculous recovery, expressing a new sense of direction and confidence in Him. Others have been motivated to seek and accept God's truths.

A prominent evangelist, Dick Mills returned from an out-of-the-body encounter with Christ, a man more able to forgive and with a new love for others. Suffering double pneumonia during a series of meetings in a Texas city, Mills was rushed to the hospital with a 105-degree temperature. At one point he passed out in the emergency room. He relates the incident this way:

> As I was falling on the floor, I heard someone say, "He's gone." And I *was* gone, for at that moment I was out of this world and getting close to the city of Heaven.
> It isn't easy for me to relate this because

it doesn't make me look good. But I have to be honest.

While the hospital staff put me in an oxygen tent and tried to induce breathing, Jesus met me, and we talked. He pointed to the city and said, "Do you know that if you go in there it's forever?" I said, "Yes. I know that one of Heaven's names is the Eternal City."

"Did you know that everything in there is based on the laws of harmony?" He probed. I replied, "Yes." "Did you know that you are out of harmony?" He continued. "Yes," I admitted.

Mills had been carrying resentment toward an individual vho had become a fierce competitor. In the ensuing conversation, Jesus reminded him of the great debt of sin for which he had been forgiven and that those sins were never again mentioned. Yet within his heart was a hurting bitterness toward the other person. Mills continues:

Jesus said, "Don't you think it would be better to go back and love that person whom you've had those feelings against?" And I said, "Yes, I really do; it would be a victory for me to go back and love that person." He replied, "I'm going to send you back."

I woke up on the fourth floor of the hospital. My wife, a registered nurse, was working to get my fever down and praying that God would send me back.

"Honey, it's no contest. It's all over. No hassle. You know that person I had a hard time loving? I love him," I whispered as I came to. "Jesus met me, and He put the love there."

Reflecting on his near-death experience, Mills says: "I found out that between this world and the next, it wasn't worth it to have all that resentment in my heart. In fact, it kept me from getting into Heaven. And I found out that when you're between worlds, your priority list all of a sudden changes. My number one priority is to be able to stand before the Lord with clean hands and a pure heart."

In some cases a God-directed, out-of-the-body experience has produced repentance of sin and a new spiritual quality in the individual. Like Godkin, Alice Harrington of Decatur, Illinois, was one of those people. Suffering from extensive injuries in a head-on car accident, she crossed the frontier into the next dimension while doctors frantically worked to save her life. Her account:

I floated to the end of the bed and sat there, watching doctors and nurses working on my broken body. I heard a nurse say, "Her blood pressure is zero and there's no heartbeat."

At that very moment, I noticed a man sitting on a chair in the corner of the room. The nurses' white uniforms and the stark white bedsheets looked yellow in comparison to the gleaming whiteness of His robe.

His hair and beard looked very, very soft and white. He wore a crown on His head and I suddenly realized He looked like the pictures I'd seen of Jesus.

"Are you Jesus?" I asked. He answered in a deep, but gentle voice. "I am the King of Kings, the Shepherd of Shepherds."

I asked if I were going to be taken and was told: "You should die now, but you have not lived for me. If you died, you could not come with me."

I hung my head in shame because I knew this was the truth. I was 29 then and even though I wasn't a wicked person, I was wild and I'd done about everything there was to do.

Even though I was terribly frightened, I asked if I could be given another chance.

"Yes," I was told, "but this time you must live for me." Then He vanished and I heard someone in the room say, "Her blood pressure's going up and I hear a heartbeat."

During the months I spent recovering, I came to realize that I was important to Jesus—as important as anyone else in the world, and I decided to change my whole way of living.[10]

Hundreds were converted to Christianity in China through the other-world testimony of a Mrs. Jang, who became a Christian in 1904 in the city of Wang Kia Kwan Dswang. The Chinese woman told this story to missionary Louisa Vaughan:

I remember seeing all the family around me crying. Then the Lord Jesus came into my room and took me by the hand and said, "Come with me!" In a short time we were before a gate of pearl. It was the gate of Heaven.

117

> We went in. I saw many beautiful houses all of pretty colors. I walked beside the Lord on the golden streets. Then we went on and I saw thousands of angels in a circle, singing and playing lovely music. In the midst was the throne of glory. The Heavenly Father sat upon it, and when I saw Him I was afraid.[11]

Mrs. Jang was allowed to come back and tell what she saw. People flocked in from miles around to hear her thrilling story. Speaking as an eyewitness, they could not reject her testimony.

Christian encounters of the heavenly kind are not illusory, for only realities can produce life-changing effects. Having been spiritually prepared by Christ is one's assurance of a God-directed experience.

In the coming chapters, I will take you on a personal adventure into the world beyond this life. While being clinically dead, I experienced the often mysterious realm of the other side, returning with new insights about life after death and with an unusual mission to fulfill.

7

From Flop to Failure

As Olive, my wife, rushed me to the hospital with the painful throb of a massive heart attack building in my chest, I prayed in agonizing defeat, "Oh, God, after a life of failure and disappointment, now this!"

And yet, in the next few days I was to see such incredible things that I could never adequately describe them. Of all people, I, Marvin Ford, was about to leave my body, travel at the speed of thought far into the other side—then return.

One of my earliest memories, somehow typical of a life of dashed hopes and rootlessness, is of rattling down a dusty Texas road in a Model T Ford overflowing with furniture, heading for yet another home, another dirt-poor farm. That Ford symbolized to me the success that could have been mine. My father was a distant cousin of Henry Ford, a lineage going back to the time when the three Ford brothers first came from Scotland. Success was almost a family characteristic.

That didn't help my father any, though. Scott Ford was a cabinetmaker—and a good one—but he just couldn't bring in enough money to support my mother and us kids. I guess the strain was too much for my parents. They broke up when I was three, and mother took us back to live with her folks.

Beulah Ford soon married again, and we moved from place to place, sharecropping. Things were bad in West Texas during the twenties. We had a depression going full swing before the rest of the country even knew what one was. We lived on farms, in little towns, anywhere we could get work.

I can remember all through my school years, working at anything I could find, just to make ends meet—milking cows, picking cotton until my fingers bled from the burrs, working in our garden, planting and plowing.

One winter we lived on a side of pork and a fifty-pound sack of black-eyed peas. That's not much for a family of seven to get by on. We'd lie awake nights, listening to the rain hammer down on our corrugated iron, leaky roof, wondering how we were going to make it through the year.

Going to school filled the hours we kids didn't work, but we had just as rough a time of it there. Being sharecroppers, we were already on the bottom rung, and to make it worse, I was just about as shy as a fawn in the woods.

Part of this shyness I owed to my stepfather. I hated him. He was from the old school and believed that children should be seen and not heard. In fact, he went further: they shouldn't even be seen unless they were called for, and I wasn't called very often.

As we walked the miles to the little three-room schoolhouse, I would shudder in anticipation of being singled out. To make things worse, my mother, who worked in a sewing factory, made all my clothes for school. She did her best, but she made the shirts to button up like girls' blouses, opposite from the way a boy's should. That really made me a laughingstock.

Because I wouldn't answer questions in class, everybody thought I was an oddball. In fact, I never did pass a single oral examination. I was just a failure, socially and academically.

Finally, I got fed up with being laughed at. I had just begun attending junior high school in Waco, and the school tough must have figured I was an easy mark because he whipped me every day after school. He was a year older than I and mean as a cornered cat. I don't know what came over me, but one day I piled in with fists flying. Next thing I knew, he was flat on his back. He just lay there on the dusty ground. I thought I'd killed him.

From that time we were friends. Now there were two toughs in school. We took on anybody in the school, with fists, sticks, rocks, anything. That cured the laughingstock problem for good.

It was about this period of my life when I found a new interest: music. Several of our neighbors played guitars, and they'd let me pick one up and plunk at it. I loved playing, and it wasn't too long before I got fairly good at it. I had a natural talent for singing, too, and soon we had a neighborhood band going.

It was great fun. We'd get out in the back yard under the clear evening sky and wail out with country music. I'd play guitar or banjo and sing; other kids would play fiddle, guitars, and we even got hold of a bass fiddle. It relieved the boredom of school three hours a day and working the rest of the time, trying to help the family through the depths of the Depression.

When I was fifteen, my stepfather left us. We had trouble in our family, partly because when he was harsh with me, my mother tried to stop him. Once I even got a gun and planned to kill him because he had abused her.

It wasn't too long before I became a school dropout and went to work full-time to help support my mother and sisters. I started out parking cars, then worked in a cafe as a hash-slinger. Finally, I ended up working in a cabinet shop—just like my father.

Our neighborhood band was getting pretty good by this time. We found a job playing in a local beer joint for fifty cents a night, plus all the beer we could drink. And I could drink a lot, having been working hard at becoming an alcoholic since I was fourteen. In fact, the free beer meant as much to me as the money, even though I was soon making more there than at the cabinet shop.

The beer joints held dances seven nights a week for all the local toughs in Waco, and our manager would drive us around to play at all the places in town. I was really on top for three or four years. Life was still hard—working sixteen to eighteen hours a day between the cabinet shop and the beer joints—but I bought my first car, had fun with the guys in the band, spent money for the first time, and even overcame my shyness . . . when I was drunk.

At the same time, though, something didn't feel right. For a while, the son of our church's head deacon—my mother always sent us kids, even if she didn't regularly attend herself—had been in our band. But it got too rough for him. My mother never knew anything about my drinking because I either spent the night with one of my buddies or came in so late she wouldn't see me. I'd walk around half the night, waiting for her to turn the lights off and go to bed.

I knew I was leading a double life. During the day I was considered a "goodie goodie," working to support my mother and sisters. At night I lived it up, having a great old time with the worst people in town. And to top it off, I faithfully attended church every Sunday, mostly because of the influence of my old grandmother. The only people in church who knew anything about my double life were those who went to the beer joints, too.

Even though everything appeared to be fine on the surface, a gnawing deep inside kept telling me something wasn't right. I can trace this feeling back to my grandmother, a really saintly woman. When I was five or six years old, she had beckoned me into her room as she lay dying and had told me how my mother had been called by God to be a missionary but had never obeyed. Instead, she'd traveled around with her father, a circuit-riding Methodist minister. My mother's mantle had fallen on me, grandmother said; I was going to be a "preacher-boy." That really scared me, because to me "mantle" meant a mantel, the heavy stone over the fireplace where I had my supper when I was bad. Her words stayed with me, eating away at my smug satisfaction and drawing me back to church each Sunday.

One Sunday when I was eighteen, I didn't make it to my church. On the way there, I passed a Pentecostal church and heard exciting singing coming from inside. The people were clapping their hands, singing at the top of their lungs and really enjoying it.

Strongly attracted to this place, I started to go in, but then stopped cold. Wasn't this big wooden barn of a building the place where the devil did his work? In fact, this was the place I had almost been arrested a couple of months before when I'd come down half-drunk one evening after playing with the band, to tell them they were of the devil. I had gotten into an argument with one of my school buddies and his father in the parking lot and had almost reached the point of working the whole bunch over. If I couldn't cast the devil out of them, I figured I'd beat him out of them!

These thoughts were racing through my mind that Sunday morning, but a tremendous power was drawing me in almost against my will. It was the same attraction that brought hundreds of people to this church every night of the week, and I wasn't so sure it was satanic.

I finally mustered the courage to open the door and peer inside. A huge crowd filled the gravel-floored building with its sawdust aisles and crude wooden platform at the front. I spotted a girl I knew from school, and just at that moment, she turned around, smiled, and motioned for me to come in and sit beside her.

With my heart pounding in fear of eternal damnation, I slid into the seat next to this freckle-faced redhead and listened hesitantly to a young girl who formed an evangelistic team with her sister, preaching the gospel hard and straight, as I'd never heard it before. I soon forgot my fears of the devil running this place. Instead I began to wonder if he was running me.

I was so caught up with what was being said that I went back every night that week to hear the truth about myself and the peace and forgiveness I could obtain from Jesus Christ. By the following Sunday evening, I was ready. One of the girls described the misery of her father's life as an alcoholic, and a stinging realization told me that was exactly where I was heading.

My uneasiness about my life kept growing until I couldn't stand it any longer. Partly out of fear, partly out of desire, I stumbled down to the front of that barn-like building, before all those people, and knelt down at the rough wooden altar. That clear spring night my toughness melted away; I accepted myself as I was and felt the flow of Jesus' love flood my whole body.

A sense of sweet release told me I had finally done the right thing. Breaking loose from my old associations was easy. My former church friends wouldn't have anything more to do with me. They figured I had joined up with the devil's gang and refused even to speak to me. As far as they were concerned, I was dead.

I did go back to the band for one night, but we had a big blow-up. I just couldn't get into the music, and they noticed I wasn't drinking.

"So what in the world is the matter with you?" one of them snapped.

"I started going to another church," I murmured. "They don't go much for this kind of stuff."

"You went to church! Don't tell me you've gone soft on us. You're acting like one of those holy rollers!"

The band leader exploded. "If that's the way you want it," he fumed, "we'll get somebody else." And that's exactly what they did.

From that time on, my whole life revolved around the church. Services were held seven nights a week for years, often lasting into the early morning. The church people figured if the devil kept the beer joints open every night, they shouldn't close down either.

During that summer, I joined a singing group in church, which we called the Faith Tabernacle Quartet. We traveled around to the churches in the area, singing in services and youth rallies every night. I never did get much sleep. I was working in the cabinet shop from seven in the morning to seven at night, then attending church the rest of the evening.

I was becoming a stronger Christian, though, and I was especially interested in this mighty spiritual power flowing through all the services. Everybody was talking about the baptism in the Holy Spirit, and I wanted to learn more. My Sunday school teacher showed me from the Bible that the baptism was a gift of God offered to every Christian who would ask.[1] It was the power that had enabled the early church to turn the world upside down, and it was that same power which drew hundreds of people every night to that humble wooden church in Waco.

This all seemed strange, but I couldn't help becoming more and more involved. I went all out for God that summer. My friends thought I had gone berserk.

By September, I was convinced that baptism in the Holy Spirit was what I needed and wanted. I went back down to the wooden altar one night, knelt in the deep sawdust, and asked Jesus to "fill me with His Spirit," as the experience also is called.

In those days, the Pentecostals "tarried" for the baptism, sometimes for weeks. A group of people crowded around me as I knelt, helping me wait. They all prayed at once. What a time we had! Some screamed in my ear, "Turn loose!" while some screamed in the other ear, "Hold on!" As soon as I learned to turn loose and hold on at the same time, I received the baptism!

That was a moment every bit as wonderful as when I had given my life to Jesus four months earlier. The power that hit me was indescribably beautiful. Tears poured down my cheeks as eternal, infinite love filled me up and overflowed. From my lips came words of an exquisite heavenly language—words I did not know and yet realized were a true language.[2] I could hardly speak English for three days.

Caught up in the beautiful experience of being filled with the Holy Spirit, I knew beyond any doubt that God was calling me into the ministry. I was sure this couldn't just be the emotion of the moment because I was totally against the idea!

"Lord," I cried, "you've made a mistake. I'm not the one you want. Don't you remember how bashful and backward I am? I could never preach. I just couldn't do it!"

On and on I went, reasoning with God. To me, the ministry meant preaching, and I knew I'd just add that to my long list of failures.

But God was persistent. Cutting through all my arguments was that same gentle, irresistible pressure: "It's you I want."

"But where will I get the money to go to school?" I asked.

"I will supply your needs," came the reply. "It's you I want."

There was nothing else I could do. I decided to go into the ministry, just as my grandmother long ago had said I would.

Through the next year I was deeply involved in the church. Our quartet was becoming well known, and we even sang on the radio occasionally. My mother and sisters had started going to church with me because they had to see for themselves what made this great change in my life. They, too, gave their lives to Christ that year.

I was beginning to lose my shyness and become more outgoing. I was singing all the time, but sometimes would stumble out a few words of testimony.

It wasn't too long before the Lord made it possible for me to go to Bible school. Joe Gerhart, who was dean of the Southern Bible Institute in Houston (now Southwestern in Waxahachie) heard our quartet sing and made us an offer: since all four of us had been called to the ministry, he would pay our tuition to his school if we would sing as part of the school's promotional program. We were so excited we could hardly wait for the semester to start.

For the next two years, I studied for the ministry at Southern Bible Institute and sang with the quartet all over Texas and the surrounding states. Things were getting better, but I was still not the "smoothest" of guys. I remember once when a girl asked me to pick up a pair of hose for her while I was in town. She handed me a stocking with which to match colors, and I stuffed it in my pocket and forgot about it.

Then, at our singing performance, I reached for a handkerchief but pulled out that long stocking, right in front of the congregation. Their laughter almost rocked the church, and it was all I could do to keep from running out the door.

Later, in 1939, our quartet became the first singing group ever to appear on television, at the San Francisco International Exposition. The exposition had a television pavilion with a studio room containing a camera about as big as an automobile. Outside was a group of receiving sets with tiny screens. We went over and said, "Hey, we're a quartet. Have you ever had a singing group on television?"

"No, we haven't," came the reply. "Come on in." We went in and performed under the hot lights. That was the high point of our trip west.

Some of my shyness had disappeared by now, but

if I tended to grow cocky, one event rudely brought me back to reality.

The first time our Bible school choir went on a singing tour, we were all told to introduce ourselves and give a short word of testimony about God's work in our lives. I hastily put together what I thought would be a dramatic speech. I intended to say, "I'm Marvin Ford from Waco. I love the fellowship of the Bible school students and the opportunity we have to minister in song to you." If that worked, I'd keep going.

I thought I'd be the first to speak, since I was singing at the end of the choir's top row. Instead, I was last, and as they went down the rows, those other kids took every word I was going to say except my name and where I was from. What was I going to do? I began to panic.

When my turn finally came, I couldn't even stand up. My legs were like wet noodles. The fellow next to me gouged me in the ribs and said, "Come on, Marvin, it's your turn." Under his prodding I struggled to my feet and squeaked, "I'm Marvin Ford from Wacoship." And sat down with a thump.

Those three hundred people nearly rolled in the aisles with laughter. I turned red and white. All my old fears came back like a flood, and at that moment I knew I would never preach. "How could you pick me, Lord?" I moaned.

From then on I was known around school as "Wacoship." Soon after that I discovered a way to minister without having to preach. Once again, music was my answer. Raymond T. Richey, a well-known evangelist in that area and founder of our Bible school, needed a song leader, and he took me on tour with him.

We traveled all over, holding city-wide

evangelistic meetings. Richey had a ministry of divine healing, and thousands of people crowded into his services. I eventually dropped out of the Bible school and toured with him from city to city, through Texas, Oklahoma, Arkansas, and Louisiana. God was using me, and I didn't even have to talk. All I had to do was play a trombone and lead singing with it.

I was able to enjoy this life for almost two years, until my mother became seriously ill. Forced to make one of the most agonizing decisions of my life, I returned home to support her. After I had finally reached some success in the Lord's work, here I was, right back where I had started.

I stayed in Waco and worked at various jobs, trying to make ends meet. All that time I was heartbroken that I couldn't serve God in a ministry. I had seen the miracles of God in Richey's services, and I prayed earnestly that He would use me in the same way. More than anything else, I wanted to have a ministry like Richey's: bringing physical and psychological healings, seeing people filled with the Holy Spirit and helping them with their spiritual problems.

I studied the passages in the Bible that described how Elisha had prayed for and received a double portion of Elijah's spirit,[3] and I prayed for a double portion of Richey's spirit to fall on me. But nothing happened.

Not being able to sit still, I began working in churches in the area anyway, as music director, minister of education, even assistant pastor. I had a moderate degree of success as long as I was playing second fiddle, but the minute I tried preaching I was a flop.

When I went to a church in Louisiana to conduct a

revival meeting, the revival dried up. Nobody would come.

I even spent a brief period as a pastor, but that didn't work either. Because I couldn't preach and couldn't minister to the people, the church lost members. God obviously wasn't blessing the ministry.

I kept trying different approaches, but it was like pounding against a brick wall. My deep longing to serve God was unfulfilled, and my call to the ministry seemed a hollow illusion. I had to face it: I was a failure.

Finally, I packed up everything I owned—which wasn't much—and headed for California. That's where people went for a new start, wasn't it? My life was a mess. In my depression, I didn't see how I could go on.

One weekend, I took a room in a run-down Hollywood hotel and determined to have it out, one way or another. Either I was going to come to terms with this grief, or I was going to kill myself.

For three days I sat in that small, bare room and drank. I didn't eat a thing, just got drunk, cried and prayed. I tried to get away from God, but I couldn't even do that.

"God," I pleaded in desperation, "you've got to take this misery out of my heart, or I'm going to end it all." And I meant it.

God knew I meant it. Suddenly I was sober—not the gradual hangover-type sobriety, but an instant, total release from my drunken stupor. The grief lifted, and God said gently, "What I have called you to, I will perform. It's you I want." No audible voice, but the words were distinctly clear in my mind, as they had been before.

My desire for suicide left, never to return. I

determined once again to trust my life to the Lord and go on. But this time I would be more cautious about plunging into the ministry I wanted so desperately to have. Maybe God's time isn't yet, I decided.

Once, while living in Oklahoma, I had learned something about the florist business. I now found an opportunity to take over a flower shop in Glendale. Three times a week I went down to the central market in Los Angeles and bought flowers for the shop. Since funerals were our best business, I developed a morbid habit of grabbing the newspaper as soon as it arrived to check the obituary column. That was how I knew how many flowers to buy.

This was a long way from the ministry, but I was moderately successful at it, if I worked eighteen to twenty hours a day. After a year and a half, though, I began spending less time in the shop because something wonderful had happened. I met the girl of my dreams.

Her name was Olive Bradley, a student at Life Bible College in Los Angeles. I met her at a meeting where Jack Holcomb, one of the members of our old quartet who had gone on to make it "big," was singing. It was amazing, but I had heard of her years earlier, when I was traveling with the quartet in her hometown of Lake Charles, Louisiana. We talked, and I offered to take her home.

"Well," she laughed, her eyes dancing, "I only live half a block from here, so you don't have very far to go!"

Instead, we went out to a malt shop and got acquainted. I just knew from that moment we would be married.

For months this delightful little girl and I saw each other nearly every night. And the nights we didn't see one another we talked interminably on the telephone. I loved everything about Olive, especially her call of God to a music ministry. Music had always rescued me from the agonies of failure, and I dreamed of us working together for the Lord.

She would be just perfect, too. She was the student body pianist and had already published a book of songs. With her popularity and my business skills, I figured we could reach together the success that had always eluded me.

At the end of that wonderful four months of getting to know each other deeply, Olive decided that I was the one for her, and we were married. We had a great start, too, holding the wedding at one of Phil Kerr's popular Monday night religious musicals at the Shakespeare Auditorium in Pasadena.

I was all ready to start going again in the music ministry; God had finally fixed everything up, and together—God, Olive and I—we would finally make the impact I had been praying for during all these years.

Our first opportunity opened up when I was asked to serve as music director for a growing church in Whittier, just outside Los Angeles. It was only part-time, but I found a job in a nearby cabinet shop to make ends meet. Everything was working out fine.

We stayed there two years, at the same time singing at the fast-growing Youth for Christ rallies. Then, we left that church to work full-time with the youth rallies, and we traveled the length of California. Olive and I made a great team: she arranged the music and played the piano, while I directed the choirs and led the song service.

Soon we added another church in Whittier to our schedule. Elated by this success, we decided that God was honoring His promise at last. Forgetting the lessons I had learned about outrunning God's timing, I decided to pack up and go back to Texas for that full-time preaching ministry I had sought for so long.

We sold our house, quit our jobs, and made the hot, dirty drive back to Texas, pulling a new house trailer. When we arrived, I searched for a position as an assistant pastor, music director, director of education—anything. As it turned out, we couldn't even give away our ministry. The old story was being told yet another time.

We held on for a couple of years, but finally decided to return to California. We served briefly again at the church in Whittier, then were asked to be music directors at an Inglewood church about thirty miles from our home. For two long years we drove back and forth between home and church, plowing through heavy Los Angeles traffic several times a week, wearing out two cars in the process.

Feeling no sense of accomplishment, I was becoming tired of the whole thing. We were more or less marking time, just living out our lives in failure. And my schedule was so hectic that I could find little time even to pray or study the Bible.

Olive, a third cousin of Mark Twain, had more success than I did. She was busy writing music, including songs and Christmas and Easter cantatas, which were published by the Gospel Publishing House. But she, too, felt the sting of failure. God had called her to a music ministry, yet all we found was rejection wherever we turned. The burden and fatigue became so great, we decided to quit.

After resigning our ministries, we began attending Christian Center (now Melodyland) in nearby Anaheim, deciding just to sit back and relax as members of the congregation, like everybody else. Maybe we'd sing in the choir, but I wasn't about to direct another one. I had done that for years, and I was worn out, physically and spiritually.

But if I intended to sit in the back row, I had picked the wrong church. Because of the blessing of God, the normal two Sunday services expanded into five. David Wilkerson came once a month. Kathryn Kuhlman held large meetings in Los Angeles once a month, too, and the Christian Center choir supplied much of the music.

Then, our song leader, Darrell Hon, started having heart trouble. The first thing I knew, I was involved in song leading again. First one service, then two, then five, plus singing in the Kuhlman choir. I was becoming even more weary, between this and my full-time job as a superintendent for a plastics company. But I also was excited, seeing the blessing of God in this church. All around me people were being given Holy Spirit ministries like healings, miracles, and the ability to teach the deeper things of God.

"Oh, Lord," I prayed, "use me, too. I don't care what it costs me."

Thirty-five years of frustration were building to a climax. God had called me, and yet that calling had not been fulfilled. Here I was, ruining my health for the Lord, but feeling no satisfaction. Failure dogged my path. These beautiful vistas of success had remained only vistas.

I didn't know it then, but my very exhaustion was to mark the turning point in my life. As I prayed to have Raymond Richey's mantle fall on me, the Lord seemed to say, "Wouldn't *my* mantle be better?" He hadn't forgotten me. He just needed to bring me to the right place of spiritual helplessness and surrender. It would not be long until an ordinary failure like me would come to have an extraordinary visit with the very One who had called—on the other side.

8

"Fatal" Heart Attack

The year 1971 began ominously. Up to this point my health had been excellent, but now problems started. They might have been expected at the age of fifty-one after years of hard work—always pushing myself to the limits, willing to tackle yet another job and miss another night's sleep. But to me it came as a surprise. I had ignored the warnings until it was too late.

My first warning came in January when I caught a terrible cold and began experiencing sharp pains in my chest and back. I went to our family doctor, Dr. J. David Rutherford, to see what he could do.

Dr. Rutherford, at that time in his late forties, is a compassionate and skilled physician, and the best family doctor I have ever had. I trusted him totally and knew he would give me a straight answer about my condition. But he could find nothing unduly alarming about my cold or pains and dismissed me with a mild prescription.

I concluded happily that I was still in good health and went back to my rigorous routine of working at the plastics mill and directing the congregational singing at Melodyland.

A few months later, however, I began having back and chest pains again. This time Dr. Rutherford took an electrocardiogram (EKG) to see if I had a heart problem.

I lay down on his examining table, and he fussed with the wires that hooked the machine to my chest. Soon the paper tape came rolling out like a long white tongue, covered with squiggles drawn by the pens that indicated my heartbeat—and my future.

"Marvin," he smiled, "I can't see anything wrong here. Your heart looks strong, very strong. Of course," he added, "this graph can't predict the future. But there is no indication of damage or any kind of problem."

"Then I can go back to work?" I asked.

"Sure," he grinned. "Just take it easy, will you?"

"Oh, you know I'll take it easy, doc," I exclaimed as I bounded off the table. We exchanged knowing grins and a few jokes, and I left the office.

Through the summer things went a little better, though I kept feeling intermittent jabs of pain, particularly when I raised my left arm higher than usual or put strain on my back and chest muscles. Fortunately, I had reached management level at work, but in spite of the fact that my job involved very little physical labor, I was under more stress than when I had been doing bench work or installation. Occasionally, I'd help unload the trucks or operate a fork lift, but my main duties were to make sure cabinets were delivered on time and to keep my men occupied.

Later in the fall, I began having problems again. This time my condition was becoming serious. My back was in almost constant pain, and I tired very easily. I could hardly even mow the lawn—two or three circles around the yard and I would be exhausted, my legs dragging.

On December 13, I was feeling so bad that I left work and went to see Dr. Rutherford again. He checked my heart with an EKG; it was negative. After giving me a quick examination and finding nothing, he said, "Marvin, I want you in the hospital for a complete checkup. Let's find out what's causing all this."

I was poked, wired, measured, and bled for the next five days at La Habra Community Hospital. Another EKG, an EMG on my spine, upper and lower GIs and enough blood tests to equal two or three transfusions were made. They also took X-rays of everything in sight. I was sure that I was going into the movies.

At the end of the ordeal, Dr. Rutherford announced, "Well, you can go home. There's nothing wrong with you—except for one thing." Then a glint came into his eyes. "No, two things: orneriness and a touch of arthritis of the spine. I can do nothing about either one, so just take it easy." Well, I knew I was born ornery, so I guess I had developed nicely through the years.

Then he added what soon was to seem grimly ironic. "I can't see anything wrong with your heart, Marvin. You have the heart of a twenty-five-year-old. If anything ever happens to you, it certainly won't be a heart attack."

I went back to work relieved, but still tired. Christmas was coming, and we were looking forward to celebrating the holidays with our friends. Yet in the midst of all the season's festivities, Olive and I felt a heavy weight of discouragement.

I had a good job and was making better money than ever before. Olive was writing music and playing for Kathryn Kuhlman. But the unknown and untreatable problem within my body was wearing me down, sapping my energy and returning only pain. Olive, too, was in pain. Arthritis had developed in her fingers, making piano-playing an agony.

Above all was the nagging sense of frustration and failure in our work for the Lord. Every day I'd pray, "Lord, how long will it be before you fulfill your promises? I'm driving myself to the grave, wasting all my energies at the mill and in church work that falls far short of what you called me to do. I'm burning the candle at both ends. When are you going to open the doors you promised? Am I ever going to see this ministry?" Since that first moment in Waco, I had known God meant to use me in an unusual ministry, but all this time, there'd been no hint.

And then there had been the personal prophecies.

Now, I never believed in prophecies of a personal nature. Oh, I knew they were in the Bible, such as when Agabus prophesied Paul's approaching imprisonment in Jerusalem,[1] but I had been taught that such things died out with the apostles.

In fact, I even had a Bible verse to prove it:

God, who at sundry times and in divers manners spake in time past unto the fathers by the prophets, hath in these last days spoken unto us by his Son, whom he hath appointed heir of all things, by whom also he made the worlds.[2]

I equated the "Son" with John 1:1: "In the beginning was the Word, and the Word was with

God, and the Word was God." Then, in John 1:14: "And the Word was made flesh, and dwelt among us. . . ." So I believed if God was going to speak to me, He would do so through His Word, not through a prophet.

And I had another pet verse, Luke 16:16, which states that "the law and prophets were until John." Thus, I concluded, the prophets died with John the Baptist in the first century. After Jesus came into the world, God began to direct us through His Word.

Unlike those who try to refute the authenticity of all the spiritual gifts in the present-day church, however, I never believed that Saint Paul in his letter to the Corinthians meant that these gifts were to diminish and eventually cease after the written Word (the New Testament) came into existence. Rather I was convinced that the disappearance of these gifts "when that which is perfect is come" referred to the second coming of Christ,[3] which has yet to take place.

Yet as I pondered the validity of these beliefs, I began to see that prophets are just as much a part of the church as are evangelists, pastors, and teachers.[4] The Bible makes no distinctions in time among these offices; if pastors are still necessary, so are prophets. Any attempt to divide the work of the Holy Spirit into ministries of the past era and ministries of the present age is unsupported by the Bible. I began to understand that the Book of Acts—being the acts of the Holy Spirit, not just of the apostles—was open-ended and continuing right down to the present moment.

Until this time, I believed that prophecy was limited to general messages of encouragement from God to a congregation, glorifying the Lord in edifying, exhorting, and comforting His people.[5]

Anything beyond this, I thought, was nothing more than fortune-telling, which is strictly prohibited by God.[6] I still believe one must be cautious in this realm. Directive prophecy must never conflict with the written Word; it must glorify God rather than man and confirm what the individual already feels within his heart.

What I did not understand was the difference between the simple gift of prophecy, which all Spirit-filled believers may exercise,[7] and the office of a prophet, which is a God-given ministry. (I would suggest Kenneth Hagin's book, *The Gift of Prophecy*,[8] for further study.)

Having accepted prophecy in general as a valid contemporary ministry, I simply was not ready to accept it when a person predicted another individual's life and future. Thus, I had some difficulty in my mind when, in 1969, recognized ministers of God began prophesying over *me*!

"You are going to lay your hands on the sick, and they will be healed," I was told. "You will see your ministry flourish around the world."

Other people told Olive and me that we would be used in the spiritual ministries of healing, detecting the activity and presence of spirits, and imparting divinely revealed insights to the people about themselves.[9] Although this confirmed what the Lord had already impressed upon me and what I longed for in my heart, I still could not accept it as coming from God. Nothing like that had ever happened in my life.

Nevertheless, my opinion on this subject began to change when Dick Mills, who has the God-given ability to combine prophecy and Bible verses in ministering to people, gave us confirmation of the previous prediction. Since I had seen his ministry confirmed over and over in people's lives, I paid rapt attention when he gave me verses as God revealed them to him.

"You will be given a new and different type of ministry," he predicted, quoting the following Bible verses:

> That he may do his work, his strange work; and bring to pass his act, his strange act.[10]
>
> The Lord shall go forth as a mighty man, he shall stir up jealously like a man of war: he shall cry, yea, roar; he shall prevail against his enemies.[11]
>
> I know thy works: behold, I have set before thee an open door, and no man can shut it: for thou hast a little strength, and hast kept my word, and hast not denied my name.[12]
>
> For a great door and effectual is opened unto me, and there are many adversaries.[13]
>
> That thine alms may be in secret: and thy Father which seeth in secret himself shall reward thee openly.[14]

To me this last verse meant that God recognized my agonizing in secret prayer for the ministry to which I had been called and that He was soon going to honor that call with a dynamic, successful ministry.

Confirmation of Mills' prophecy poured in over the next three years. One person saw me in a vision, running up and down hills in a far-off country. That has already been fulfilled more than once!

A friend known for her prophetic gift said she saw a ministry spanning the globe, with miracles being performed as we traveled.

Chuck Flynn, who has a worldwide prophetic ministry, saw me as Aaron, who was anointed with oil that ran down his beard and flowed over his garment, covering him totally in the anointing of the Lord.[15] He said we would manifest God's power to His people.

Another minister, Leland Davis, later confirmed Dick Mills' quotations regarding the open doors and the miracles that would glorify God.

And Dick Joyce, still another with the gift of prophecy, gave us two more Bible verses:

> I will go before thee, and make the crooked places straight: I will break in pieces the gates of brass, and cut in sunder the bars of iron: and I will give thee the treasures of darkness, and hidden riches of secret places, that thou mayest know that I, the Lord, which call thee by thy name, am the God of Israel.[16]
>
> Ye shall go out with joy, and be led forth with peace: the mountains and the hills shall break forth before you into singing, and all the trees of the field shall clap their hands.[17]

Even for someone who doubted personal prophecy, these and other predictions by different people—sometimes those who didn't even know us or our background—came together like a solid structure. We became convinced that God had something prepared for us, yet we still hadn't seen it. Rather than inflating our egos, such pronouncements only deepened our confusion as, like Jesus' mother, Mary, we pondered these things in our hearts until God's time for fulfilling them.

With these thoughts weighing heavily on us, we went through Christmas of 1971, not knowing that a day of events soon to follow would make all these promises seem empty and false.

December 29 dawned clear and pleasantly cool. If we hadn't been so busy at work, I might have been able to appreciate the day's beauty. We were behind schedule, frantically keeping three or four rush jobs going at once, and I was responsible for getting everything out on time.

I arrived at work early that morning, half an hour before my men came. By ten o'clock, we were ready to haul the laminated plastic tops from the next building for installation on our cabinets. Everybody on my crew was so busy, I decided to transfer the material myself.

I piled the heavy cabinet tops onto a four-wheel cart and started easing them down the steep slope in front of the plastics building. About halfway down the slope, the cart hit a rock, and those slick plastic tops began sliding off, heading directly for my boss's catamaran. In a flash I realized that besides damage to the boat, nothing could justify the time and expense needed to reconstruct those tops.

With a sudden burst of strength, I reached out and grabbed them. As my hands closed around the tops, I felt a stabbing pain in my chest as if an elephant had stomped on it. I bent over in agony as the pain traveled through my neck and up into the lower jaw. My strength drained away momentarily, then began to return—slowly. Holding on to the cabinet tops, I waited until the pain subsided to a dull ache.

Hesitantly, I straightened up and pushed the cart the remaining distance to our building. My body began to feel cold. "Probably getting the flu," I reasoned, refusing to admit what was happening.

In the next thirty minutes I downed six aspirins, hoping they would relieve the growing pain. I began to have difficulty breathing. I forced myself to take deep breaths, having heard that this is the way to keep from passing out when severe chest pains strike. The cardiologist later told me this was probably what kept me from dying before I got to the hospital.

Realizing I wasn't getting better, I staggered over to the main office and fell onto a stool, supporting my chin with my right hand. I tried to bring up my left hand to help with the support, but it wouldn't move. I reached over to pick it up with the good hand just as my boss walked in.

"What the - - - - is wrong with you?" he boomed.

"I think I've got the flu. I feel pretty sick," I answered weakly.

"Man, you're in bad shape. You'll have to go home," he said sympathetically.

One of the other fellows offered to drive me, but old stubborn Marvin wouldn't hear of it.

"No, you don't need to drive me," I groaned. "I'll drive myself home."

Seeing the futility of argument, they reluctantly let me go, making me promise I would pull over and lean on the horn if I couldn't make it. I drove slowly through the heavy traffic, somehow making the five miles home. Arriving just before noon, I entered through the back door, took my jacket off, and fell across the bed. Just as I did, the pain became so intense I started to sob for the first time in my adult life. Olive took one look at my white, sweating face and ran to the telephone.

"Get him to the hospital, quick!" ordered Dr. Rutherford. "Take him to emergency."

In two or three minutes Olive was ready, and we were on our way to the La Habra Community Hospital, darting in and around traffic as fast as she could drive. We covered the three miles in moments and squealed up to the emergency entrance.

Leaning heavily on Olive, I shuffled through the double doors into emergency and stood there while she talked with the nurse. They brought a wheelchair for me and began calling around for a room to put me in.

Olive's Irish temper exploded. "Can't you see he's about ready to pass out?" she fumed. "You get him into a room right away and do something! He could die sitting there in that wheelchair. There are lots of vacant beds!" Although she had not seen a heart attack before, she had suspected almost from the minute I came home what it was. She had never before seen me cry in pain.

After a seemingly endless wait, a nurse arrived with a bed; they transferred me to it and moved me into one of the nearby rooms. Three nurses worked steadily over me. One was attaching suction cups to my chest for the EKG machine, while the other two tried to read my pulse and blood pressure.

"Don't get excited," I said teasingly to Maria, a black nurse I had gotten to know during my hospital stay two weeks before. "Take it easy; I'm all right."

The look on her face told me she didn't agree. "What's the matter, Maria?" I asked lightly. "Isn't your blood pressure machine working?"

"It's working all right," came the tight-lipped reply.

Nothing more was said, but I could tell by the nurses' faces and actions that something was seriously wrong. They ignored my efforts at banter and worked on feverishly. The nurse searching for my pulse felt all over my arm and then dug both hands into the upper part of my neck, under my jaw. With fear in her eyes, she jabbed a silent finger in the direction of the intensive care unit (ICU) down the hall.

The nurse hooking up the EKG machine immediately ripped the suction cups off my chest, and the three of them pushed the rolling bed down the hall at a full run.

All this time, the elephant was pounding on my chest, but I didn't realize how sick I really was.

Arriving at the ICU, I was connected to a cardiac monitor, which looks like a little television set, and an oxygen tube put up my nose. Although the nurses hadn't been able to find any pulse, the monitor detected it and gave a reassuring beep and a little red flash of light with every heartbeat. It also displayed a squiggle on its small screen—much like the graphs I had drawn in school when I was a kid—to show everyone that I really was alive.

I began to look around the small cubicle in which I was confined, wondering what would happen next. On the wall over my head was the faithful heart monitor, beeping happily. The oxygen tube ran from my nose into a hookup in the wall, and on the other side of my bed was the intravenous feeding apparatus (IV) they knew I would soon be needing.

Gazing past the people crowded around my bed, I could look from my corner room into the large central area of the ICU. In its center was the long console or nurses' station, which held small screens duplicating the squiggles of each patient's heartbeat on his own monitor. Above the console was a large clock, clearly visible from my cubicle, and nearby were five more beds for less critical patients.

When Dr. Rutherford came in at a run, he grabbed

my arm without so much as a "hello" and felt for a pulse. He found none. Ordering a shot of morphine to ease my pain, he asked gruffly, "What happened to you? Are you trying to make a liar out of me?"

"I'd go to any length to make a liar out of my doctor," I replied with a wink.

"Well, you sure did." He ordered the IV and located the faint vein which eluded the nurse. "Now tell me everything that happened, in detail," he commanded.

When I finished, he shook his head. "Boy, you've had a good one."

I tried my best to joke with him, but I was becoming light-headed and disoriented. During the afternoon, a friend of ours whom Olive had called came in and prayed for me, then left to contact others to pray. It was obvious that I was getting worse.

After several hours of working with me, Dr. Rutherford revealed that he was having a bout with pneumonia himself.

"Either I'm going to go home, or you'll have to move over and make room for me," he smiled. I put my hand on him as he left, and asked the Lord to touch him. He must have done it, for the doctor returned later that evening.

During the afternoon, several more of our friends came in to pray for me, and the nurses began to be irritated by all this traffic. By six o'clock everyone had left, including an exhausted Olive after getting the nurse to promise to call if anything happened.

I slept under the morphine until about ten o'clock that night, when I was awakened by a dreadful stirring in my chest. My heart felt like it was pounding its way up into my throat. The rhythm was wildly erratic as I began fibrillating; my pulse and heartbeat were completely uncoordinated.

Suddenly, my faithful cardiac monitor sounded a piercing buzz—indicating that my heart had stopped—and the room was filled with doctors and nurses. Dr. Rutherford rushed in with Dr. Harry Riegel, the cardiologist, and they began to work feverishly on me. Dr. Riegel ordered adrenalin shot directly into my heart. Sinking a needle that looked like a sixteen-penny nail straight through my ribs didn't solve the problem, so he doubled up his fist and slammed me in the chest as hard as he could.

The pain was so intense I could barely stand it, but my heart started beating regularly again. They gave me two more shots of morphine to ease the agonizing pain, but morphine just makes me want to climb the walls. I forced myself to close my eyes and relax as the doctors stepped outside my cubicle.

They must have thought I was asleep, but I overheard clearly as Dr. Riegel whispered, "Jim, there is no further need for me to return on this case. He will start fibrillating again. The patient cannot live through the night and probably for not more than two hours."

"I wouldn't bet on it. We'll wait and see," Dr. Rutherford mused.

What would you do if you heard that? Uh huh, I did too! I prayed!

"If this is it, Lord," I cried, "I know I'm ready to meet you. We settled that long ago, but what about all the prophecies that have been given to us? Won't these people be called false prophets?"

With the memory of those predictions vivid in my mind, it was difficult to reconcile the fact I had been given up for dead. Dr. Rutherford returned to my bedside and gave me his diagnosis: an acute inferior myocardial infarction. As he explained it, the main artery leading from the back of the heart muscle had an infarction; in layman's language, I call it a "blowout." The flow of blood had stopped, and the heart muscle began forming scar tissue. Since the muscle wouldn't work, naturally it couldn't pump the blood. They had to give me stimulants to keep the remaining portion of my heart beating and the blood flowing.

"And how are you feeling, doc?" I asked with all the cheer I could muster after this news.

"I'm feeling fine again," he smiled reassuringly.

"I prayed for you while you were gone."

"Well, good," he said. "I'm glad somebody did."

After a while he went home again, and I slept the rest of the night. Well, almost. I tried to get up to go to the bathroom once, contrary to orders. Because of the sedation, I didn't realize what I was doing. I took the oxygen out of my nose, the needle out of my arm, and was detaching the cardiac monitor from my chest when three nurses converged on me in fury and threw me back into bed. It would be some time before I had that much spunk again.

Early the next morning, Thursday, Olive returned, and the nurses told her what a "bad boy" I had been. My skin had begun turning a yellowish green and was stretched tightly over my bones, making me look like a masked Halloween skeleton. There was no way I could hide the seriousness of my condition.

"I've been calling all over the country, asking people to pray for you," Olive said tenderly.

I was glad of that. There also had been plenty of visitors to pray for me, and that caused quite a stir in the ICU, which is normally restricted to the immediate family.

The nurse's aide at the front desk accosted Olive

and said, "Mrs. Ford, I have to talk with you a moment. There are entirely too many people coming in to see your husband. He is under intensive care, and we can't allow any more visitors except very close family members and one clergyman. Who are all these people going in? They claim to be clergy. I don't understand this."

"They are clergy," she replied. "The reason we have so many is that we are well known around here, having sung, played, and ministered in so many churches. All these people have heard about Marvin, and they want to come in."

"Well, I'm sorry. You'll have to eliminate all but one. You name whomever you wish."

Olive came in and told me this. "Have you called Pastor Wilkerson?" I asked.

She shook her head. "I know he's so busy."

"Go call Ralph," I urged. She did and learned that he was expected back from Texas that afternoon and would be notified immediately of my serious condition.

Olive went home for a few hours, and I rested. Early in the afternoon, I noticed a strange wall of blackness floating hazily near the ceiling at the left-hand side of my room. As I watched in fascination, the darkness started moving over toward me, blanking out that whole side of the room. It came closer and closer as I watched, flickering back and forth over me, as if deciding whether to go on, and then filling the remainder of the room. I didn't know what it was, but I sure didn't like it.

As the blackness reached the full extent of the room, I became dimly aware of my cardiac monitor shrieking out its awful buzzing sound. My heart had failed again, and this time my veins had also

151

collapsed. Because the heartbeat had become so weak, it could no longer pump blood through my body. There was no blood pressure to keep the veins open.

In a moment, the nurses were over me, working frantically to keep me alive. One was sticking a hypodermic needle into my stomach, and another was trying to find a functioning vein for the IV medication. Soon, the blackness receded from the room, and I began to help the nurse find a vein.

"Try the back of my hand," I suggested feebly. "Twist the needle into one of those tough veins, and it should go right in."

"Are you trying to tell me how to do this?" she asked, relieved that I was conscious. "I've been doing this for years."

"I'm a cabinetmaker," I persisted. "When screws won't go in, we just get them right up to where they're supposed to go and then twist them in real quick."

She tried it, and sure enough, it worked! My veins opened again, and the cardiac monitor settled down to its steady beeping. I've heard Olive play Bach, Beethoven, and all the great music, but the most beautiful melody I've ever heard was the quiet, steady beeping of that monitor.

Olive came back a short time later, but they didn't tell her anything. She knew, though, that I was worse than they were letting on because they cut the visiting time down from five minutes an hour to two minutes an hour or less. Yet she was calm, trusting that the Lord would fulfill His promises. She knew I was not going to die.

About six o'clock I saw Pastor Wilkerson stick his head in the door, but the nurse wouldn't let him in. I could hear the commotion outside.

"I'm Pastor Wilkerson—"

"Nobody's permitted in here," she answered curtly. "We're busy."

"I'm not here to visit," Ralph answered patiently. "I'm here on a mission."

"Well, you're not coming in! You'll have to wait an hour because his wife just left."

"I'm sorry, but I *am* coming in."

"If you try, Reverend, I'll call the security guard!"

"Go ahead and call the guard. I am a minister and have a right to come in here. The family called me, so I am responding to their call. I'm sorry, but I'm going in!"

"You'll go in over my dead body," she stormed, heading for the telephone.

Moments later the guard approached. "What's the problem?"

"This minister is trying to force his way in here, and I've told him he can't come in! This patient needs medical help right now. He doesn't need a pastor," she snapped.

Olive had been standing in the hall and offered to call Dr. Rutherford. The security guard, who is a Christian, walked with Ralph to the head office to await word from the doctor.

The next thing I knew, Ralph was marching into my room. I learned later that Dr. Rutherford had told the switchboard operator, "Ralph Wilkerson's presence in that room is as important as mine, if not more important."

"Let Reverend Wilkerson in," I heard the guard command. So Ralph and the guard entered as the nurse grumbled, "Well, all right, but I think it's ridiculous!"

Relating this story in his book, *Beyond and Back*, Wilkerson comments:

This much resistance is not normal. I sensed this was spiritual opposition, not just a stubborn nurse.

Nurses don't resist a preacher; they're trained not to react against ministers. Doctors and nurses in hospitals have been considerate in working with pastors, and I've attended seminars where hospital chaplains trained pastors on how to visit the sick.

At some point you have to be determined not to let people tell you what to do. You move on when you know it's a command of God. It was that determined faith that made me push ahead.

I could see the color of death on Marvin, and the smell of death was in the room. When I walked into the room, I could actually feel a spirit of opposition.[18]

"How are you doing?" Pastor Wilkerson began as he approached my bed.

"I'm pretty sick," I moaned.

"I know. But in my spirit I also know you'll be all right," he reassured.

As the nurses gave me oxygen, we had prayer. Yet I grew weaker. I stared out at my little world through deeply sunken eyes. I knew heart patients either get better or they get worse and die. There is no middle ground. At that moment, I realized I was definitely getting worse. Only my trust in the Lord—and the comfort of those prophecies—kept me going.

Friday afternoon the dreaded black wall returned. Again, it crept in from the left side of the room, hovering and moving back and forth over my body for a short while before filling the room. I was aware that death and life were waging warfare over my body. At times the light would gain, but suddenly the dismal darkness prevailed again, and all was as black as night.

The music of my cardiac monitor changed to a dissonant buzz, and my veins collapsed a second time. Again, the nurses worked over me, frantically trying to restore life to my body. They were practically making a sieve out of my hands, attempting to reopen the veins. I thought if they ever got my blood pressure up I'd spray the whole room with blood. The nurses finally succeeded, but I was more critical than ever. By now my body color was ash gray.

The next morning was New Year's Day, 1972, and Olive came early to feed me breakfast. Both of us were concerned about the prophecies. On the one hand, we knew that prophecies, though messages from God, are delivered through imperfect human channels. Many people have gotten into trouble in the past by accepting personally directed predictions at face value, without testing them as the Bible directs.[19] Had we been misled?

Yet, on the other hand, we *had* tested the prophecies. They confirmed what the Lord had already been telling me, and because so many of them were from different people of God, we ruled out the possibility of coincidence.

Perplexed and searching for an answer, somehow we felt this first day of the new year might hold the answer. I certainly couldn't get much worse and live. My speech was a barely audible whisper, and it was very difficult for me even to move.

Olive had gone home for a while, and I was lying on

the bed, vaguely aware of the low murmuring of the nurses, when that horrible black wall appeared again at the left side of the room and began its deadly crawl toward my bed.

"Oh, no, not again," I moaned. It seemed like the Angel of Death was coming to claim me. "Lord, I'm tired of that," I whined. "Don't let it come."

It kept coming. I could still hear the nurses and the beeping of the monitor, but they faded slowly as the black wall advanced. Finally, it hovered over me. It was like being in the Carlsbad Caverns of New Mexico, where they take you deep into the earth and briefly turn off all the lights. You can feel the darkness, it is so thick.

Unknown to me, at this same moment Pastor Wilkerson was in his office, preparing his Sunday morning message. Here's how he relates it:

> Suddenly I felt directed by the Holy Spirit to go to the La Habra Community Hospital and pray for Marvin again. Heading straight for ICU, I did not meet opposition this time. The doctor had left orders to let me in anytime.
>
> Mrs. Ford had just left, weary with hours of waiting and sleeplessness. The nurse let me into the room. I walked to the bed in the corner, pulling the curtain about us. [20]

But the moment Pastor Wilkerson was praying, I had already journeyed to the other side.

My vision had faded into blackness, as I tried to focus my eyes on the wall clock in the ICU—to hold on to the last shreds of consciousness. It was about 2:10 P.M.

"Lord, I'm tired of fighting," I sighed. "I'm ready to go. Into your hands I commend my spirit."

The black wall gathered momentum and eclipsed the entire room. I heard the monitor begin its insistent buzz, and I could feel something stir deep within my spirit.

The room of the hospital suddenly seemed to disappear, and I shot up like a rocket, climbing in a northerly direction at an incredible rate of speed.

In what seemed but a moment, I was deep in the blackness of space, heading for a brilliant white light. As I drew closer, its radiance grew almost beyond the limits of endurance. Suddenly, I was enveloped by the light and hovered over the most magnificent city I had ever seen. My spirit had left its now cold body far behind in that hospital bed. I had traveled to the other side. What I saw and heard there is almost impossible to put into words.

9

A City Among the Stars

At the end of 1972, brisk winds had cleared the Christmas skies of Los Angeles, and I was alive and descending with Olive in a Boeing 747 jumbo jet over the vast Southern California metropolis. Olive motioned excitedly for me to peer out the window.

The plane dipped its wing slightly as if to accommodate our view of the spectacular scene below. "Is this what Heaven looks like?" she beamed.

My spirit leaped within. As far as we could see, multicolored Christmas lights—blue, yellow, green, orange and red—mingled with the city's white glow.

"Ooooeeee, look at that!" I laughed, barely able to contain myself. "Honey, just visualize this about a million times more beautiful, and that is what Heaven looks like!"

How else can I describe that huge space metropolis bursting with dazzling, yet delicate hues of rainbow light? Heaven, as the city often is called, is just as the Bible depicts it—and more.[1]

Here is my experience of it when I sped "like a rocket" from my hospital bed.

Jasper Walls and Pearl Gates

From my vantage point high above that heavenly metropolis, I could see massive jasper walls stretching far into the distance. Surrounding the city, the transparent walls reflected a brilliant yellow-green light, which mingled harmoniously with the multicolored hues of gem-studded foundations. Inset at regular intervals, three on each side of the city, were gates of pearl, each gate a beautiful solid round pearl a hundred or more miles in diameter. Astonishingly, shadows do not exist, for a delicate transparency prevails throughout Heaven.

With my first glimpse, I was awed not only at Heaven's splendor, but its size. Large enough to accommodate billions of people,[2] the city stretches approximately fifteen hundred miles in each direction, including up.[3] Vision is unlimited on the other side and, hovering hundreds of miles above its base, I could see all around the city and to its lower regions.

As I drew closer, the walls faded into the distances. Millions of small sparkling lights came into view, which appeared to be dancing gracefully in perfect harmony, singing melodies more beautiful than man has ever heard. For a moment it seemed I had become one of those lights and joined them in song. I could understand the lyrics of this heavenly tongue.

Dazzling Light

My attention was attracted toward a dazzling white light radiating from the center of the city. Its brilliance made the other lights pale by comparison. Imagine looking into the center of a searchlight like the ones used to advertise grand openings and other special events. The resplendent aura surrounding God's throne is infinitely more radiant than one of these several-million-candlepower beams. A huge rainbow arched above the light like a crowning dome. It is impossible to describe, for besides the seven colors reflected by a prism—red, orange, yellow, green, blue, violet and indigo—I saw hues that do not exist on Earth.

Many joyous splendors await those who pass through the gates of pearl. What scene flashes to your mind at mention of the word paradise? Beautiful parks with picturesque landscapes, cool flowing streams and crystal pools, wooded nooks, fragrant flowers of every variety and color, caroling birds, and playful animals romping in unwilting meadows?

Let us view some of these wonders not only through my eyes but those of others who either have seen visions of the other side or have returned from the beyond to describe what they saw.

Adullan Children

In the early 1900s a great spiritual awakening took place in the Adullan Home for Children in Kotchiu, a tiny town in the Yunnan Province of China. During this revival the beggar children caught spectacular glimpses of the heavenly city. Although having no background in the Bible, what they saw bears striking resemblance to the biblical account and to that of other witnesses.

In rapid flight through space, they marveled at the beauty of stars, sparkling like the million lights of a huge metropolis viewed from a mountain top. As they sped more deeply into space, a star brighter than any other appeared in the distance, growing larger and larger until the whole universe seemed resplendent in its radiance.

Within moments, the children were in sight of the heavenly city, its jasper walls scintillating with varying shades of yellow, blue, cream, green, variegated, red, purple and violet.

Seen at a distance, the space metropolis appeared to be three cities in one, each suspended above another. The largest below and the smallest at the top formed a pyramid. The children learned that God's throne is in the upper region. This corresponds with what I saw. Approaching the city from a different angle, I noticed three levels, each more spectacular than the other in ascending splendor.

The Adullan boys reported that they were welcomed at the pearly gates by angels shining in flawless white. Inside, the streets were golden and filled with angels singing, rejoicing, playing harps, dancing, and praising God. Escorted through parts of the city, the children saw brilliant jeweled houses, filled with golden furnishings, opening onto transparent golden streets.

The boys also visited a paradise area, a common experience of many who tour Heaven. That such a place exists within the city is clearly taught by the Bible, "To him that overcometh will I give to eat of the tree of life, which is in the midst of the paradise of God" and "Today shalt thou be with me in paradise."[4] There the children saw trees bearing delicious fruit, touched flowers of infinite beauty and color, smelled the delightful fragrances of their blooms, listened to exotic birds, and romped on manicured carpets of rich green grass.[5]

Artist's Delight

It is impossible to paint a detailed heavenly scene,

but some descriptions include stately mansions with infinite varieties of architectural marvels set in exquisite parks, vast fields of blooming, fragrant flowers, incredible mountain ranges dense with evergreen, great gorges with stupendous cataracts, bright meadows, groves of giant trees hanging with golden fruit, broad avenues lined by blooming shrubs, gushing fountains—an endless variety of lush landscapes.

According to those who have visited the world beyond, paradise plains exist on all levels of the city, each arranged in ascending degrees of grandeur. The most magnificent scene stretches before the immense throne of God. No other region anywhere in the universe compares with the glories of this realm.

How many plains decorate the heavenly landscape is unknown, for glimpses of the city—whether in spirit or by vision—have been limited. The mystery deepens as some return with instructions not to reveal what they saw or heard in this city of the beyond. Such was the case with the Apostle Paul.[6] Much of what I heard and experienced cannot yet be told. Indeed, no portrait of the city comes close to the marvels awaiting those who depart this life prepared by Christ, for no one has seen the city in its entirety, nor can human vocabulary capture the dimensions of the other-world reality.

Infant Paradise

The various plains of the city are similar, though differing in beauty and detail. Marietta Davis identifies one as an infant paradise.

She viewed a magnificent instruction temple of multidimensional grandeur surrounded by Eden-like beauty. In this part, velvety green lawns

162

stretch widely under clumps of exotic trees and among fragrant flowering shrubs and blossoming vines. Water fountains tinged with gold are scattered here and there along wending pebbled, marbled, or golden walks lined by flowers of every hue. Birds of delicate colors and varying sizes flitted among the trees and swooped in chirping ballets to delight the children who romped under the watchful care of teacher-angels.

A spiraling, gently flowing river, bordered on either side by a golden avenue with trees, shrubs and flowers, circles the plain—intersecting twelve times to divide the park into 144 sections. Bridges of magnificent architecture span the crystal clear waters at each boulevard crossing. Beds of gorgeous flowers set in fields of lush green grass as soft as silk fill the air with their delicate perfume. In each of the sections, palaces of indescribable grandeur are set back from each boulevard and avenue-bordered river. The palaces or temples of instruction in the outer sections are of lesser splendor, graduating in glory as they approach the main temple in the center.

Marietta said each section contains fifty-seven mansions set in separate parks. Residences for children, these homes vary in architecture as the parks around them differ in arrangement and beauty. Each estate is harmoniously suited to the building it surrounds.

The paradise plains differ one from another in detail as well. Some are mountainous with picturesque valleys and plateaus similar to the rolling lawns of spacious golf courses.[7]

Golden Lake

Another who visited the world beyond describes a

glass-smooth lake resembling a sea of molten gold. Blossoming and fruit-bearing trees grow down to its shoreline in many places. The following account of this lake and its surroundings is given by Rebecca Springer in *Within the Gates*:

> In many places and far, far away across its shining waters arose the domes and spires of what seemed to be a mighty city. Many people were resting upon its flowery banks, and on the surface of the water were boats of wonderful structure, filled with happy souls, and propelled by unseen power.
>
> Above we saw a band of singing cherubs, floating high overhead. As we watched, groups of children played around in joyous freedom, and there were happy shouts of laughter that echoed over the lake.[8]

Sweet Fruit and Perfumes

General William Booth spoke of a bank of roses growing like a multicolored blanket under towering fruit trees that lined a crystal clear river. He could pick and taste the fruit, which he described as "sweet beyond all earthly sweetness," while the surrounding atmosphere was heavy with the sweet odors of luxuriant blossoms.

"The air was filled with the sweet perfume of the flowers," another witness confirmed. "Birds were singing gaily, and little brooks tinkled merrily through ferns, flowers and trees. After walking for a while, we came to a gorgeous palace. My eyes were blinded for a moment at its grandeur."[9]

It is impossible to conjure the mingling aromas of heavenly perfumes. But capture for a moment the delicate scents of hyacinth, roses, carnations, lilacs, lilies, magnolias, gardenias, and all of Earth's sweetest floral extracts. These are only hinting breezes wafting from the other side to tantalize our unrefined senses. But in the jeweled city beyond, we will enjoy the infinite capacity to distinguish and appreciate ten thousand perfumes permeating the atmosphere.

Heavenly Housing

Many descriptions are given of heavenly housing, indicating a wide spectrum of architectural wonders in varying degrees of grandeur and size. Some homes are small, golden one-room apartment units garnished by sparkling jewels, often seen paralleling golden streets row upon row. Those I viewed resembled miniature thrones, none of which contained bedrooms. Other dwellings are described as elegant houses or stately mansions, some with domes supported by massive columns, each set in exquisite estates and basking in a golden, rosy aura like the afterglow of a southern sunset in midsummer.

Various types of contruction materials include transparent gold and combinations of ivory, highly polished marbles and rare woods. The dwellings often are described as lavishly decorated with gold and silver and garnished with settings of diamonds, pearls, emeralds, and every other precious stone known to man. The woods are of incredible beauty, hue and fine texture, and the gems sparkle in the brilliant golden light of the city.

Other Realities

Many are the exciting portraits of Heaven, but none is more thrilling than its other realities. One of these is light.

In this dimension of afterlife, light prevails in the presence of night. While darkness exists in the physical realm wherever the sun does not shine, the spiritual plane coexists in radiant day—a spiritual light which cannot be detected by the human eye, except by supernatural vision or by the spirit when out of the body. This brings Psalm 139:12 sharply into focus: "Yea, the darkness hideth not from thee; but the night shineth as the day: the darkness and the light are both alike to thee."

Seneca Sodi is one who noted the phenomenon:

> I found that my vision was greatly improved since being freed from the mortal body—nor did I regret now I was released, for everything seemed to shine with a luster and glow with a brightness I had never known before; and what seemed more remarkable still was that the sunlight did not aid me in any sense to comprehend things about me, for I knew that at night when all the world were asleep and that it was entirely dark to outward human eyes, yet to me everything shone with a splendor more grand than the brightest noonday Earth ever afforded.[10]

Every house, street, tree, flower, river, and mountain in Heaven is the embodiment of this brilliance. Auras of rainbow hues surround every person and angel in the city, so resplendent no mortal can look upon them. Having life-giving properties, the light appears to emanate from the individual, though it is a reflection of the great splendor coming from the center of the city. Varying

according to the spiritual attainment of the person,
the aura gives one the appearance of being dressed
in flawless white, while at the same time clothed in
beautiful colors of varied hues.

Those living on the higher planes of the city
radiate the brightest light, being so resplendent that
their glory must be cloaked so others of lower degree
can look upon them. Visiting the higher levels is
possible, but the spirits of lower realms must be
prepared or covered so they can stand in the
presence of greater glory. Perhaps this partially
explains the degree of rewards awaiting those who
make the ultimate journey beyond.

Another remarkable phenomenon is the speed of
communication and travel.

Sounds inaudible to the physical ear can be heard
by the spirit. Thought transference (mental
telepathy) and clairaudience (hearing voices in the
mind) are not unique to the occult world, but are
common means of communication in all realms of the
other side. Marietta Davis explains the phenomenon
this way:

> They spoke and no audible utterance
> attended, yet thought moved with thought,
> and spirit was familiar with the mind of
> spirit. Ideas associated with their heavenly
> life, flowed from being to being, and soon I
> learned that in Heaven there is no
> concealment.[11]

Comprehension is as swift as thought, and
language barriers do not exist in Heaven. What
would take years for the human mind to understand,
is captured here in a fleeting moment.

Heaven is not a silent world. Thought

transference is only one means of communication. Many witnesses have heard the caroling of birds, the majestic anthems of angels, and the orchestrated crescendos of harmonic symphonies. Many report the audible conversations of angels and loved ones. Some have heard the voice of Jesus.

Travel in the heavenly afterlife can be as slow as a leisurely stroll or as swift as the speed of thought. My flight to the stars seemed as quick as the snap of a finger. In this magnificent city speed is rapid without hurry—or leisurely without delay.

The city's residents can "drift" through the air, take slow walks, jog, or catch a ride on a "chariot of light," the latter indicating some form of vehicular traffic. Only a few moments are needed, witnesses say, for the "wings of light" to bear a spirit to Heaven, though most seem to travel there and back without an other-world spaceship. Could these "chariots" or "wings of light" account for some of today's UFOs, coming to carry departed souls to the jeweled city?

Heaven also is a gourmet's paradise. Some say they have seen vast stretches of vegetable gardens, countless fruit orchards and gorgeous banqueting halls filled with tables spread with delectable foods. Incredible? Little difference exists between the physical and spiritual worlds, except the dimensions they represent and the degree of glory attained. What God created on Earth in its perfect state, He first introduced to the world beyond. We see on Earth only the image of other-world realities.

Eating and drinking on the other side is not for satisfying a craving or maintaining one's existence. It is for the pleasure of taste and the development of spiritual life and perception. Heavenly fruits, particularly from the Tree of Life, have spiritual properties that expand one's capacity for knowledge and understanding.

That these fruits are real, not figurative, is evident in the testimonies of witnesses. One reports, "The fruits . . . are of a finer flavor than mortals ever tasted, and they have a life-invigorating power adapted to Heaven." Rebecca Springer noted one fruit resembled a "Bartlett pear, only much larger and infinitely more delicious. . . . Another variety was in clusters, the fruit also pear-shaped, but smaller than the former, and of the consistency and flavor similar to the finest frozen cream."[12] Others describe one of the twelve fruits of the Tree of Life as similar to tropical breadfruit. Still another fruit resembles a transparent grape and is said to open one's understanding to the mysteries of the heavenly afterlife.

Water from the River of Life, which flows from the throne of God through the center of the city into countless tributaries and springs, also has life-invigorating properties. Permanent dwellers of the jeweled city must pass through the river's depths to be cleansed from the taints of mortality and become acclimated to the heavenly atmosphere. Drinking of the water is not for quenching thirst, but to enlarge one's capacity for life.

A thousand years would not be long enough to experience just a small portion of that city. One will never comprehend its total dimensions and splendor. Yet in that world without weariness, weakness, or sickness, hearing will be so perfected we can note the finest sounds and deepest tones; smell will be so refined we can detect a million perfumes that Earth has never known; sight will be so unrestricted we can see a million miles as clearly as the hand before us; taste will be so keen that the delicate flavors of heavenly desserts will dance upon our tongues in sheer delight, and feeling will be so sensitive we can experience the deepest depths and the loftiest heights of Christ's exhilarating joy.

Mind, too, will be perfected on the other side. We'll not only think rapidly, but accurately, and retain perfect memory. Knowledge not only will continue to expand, but we'll see things in true perspective, and our sense of intuition will reach its ultimate.

Worship and being in the presence of Christ, however, is the greatest glory of Heaven. Jesus is the life of the city. His glory shines from the throne; His life pulsates from the throne. Heaven's harmony is directed from the throne. All that ever was, is, and shall be finds birth at the throne. And it was to this realm I felt drawn as the millions of sparkling lights danced and sang below me.

Enough of Him to Go Around

God had a purpose for my visit: an encounter with the shining light that I sensed was Jesus.

Approaching the throne, I passed through a maze of rainbow colors that seemed to prepare me for the splendors of this region. God appeared as an intense, enveloping light. To His right was another penetrating light, somewhat oval shaped, which completely captured my adoration. Although I could not distinguish any of His features because of the brightness, I recognized this light as Jesus.

Intuitively, I knew His expression was one of supreme tenderness and love. At no time did I touch Him, but fell prostrate at His feet in worship.

At that moment His entire attention focused on me, and I was welcomed into His presence as though I were the only one there.

170

"Lord, how can it possibly be that there are billions in Heaven and on Earth who would like a little of your attention, and you're giving it all to me?" I marveled.

"My son, don't you know there is enough of me to go around?" His reply flashed in my mind.

Although I have longed to see Jesus as others have, that encounter and His words were so fulfilling, I am content to wait until the day He has appointed for my ultimate journey to the other side.

Words do not exist that can capture His portrait. Yet witnesses from the beyond have brought back fascinating descriptions of His likeness. In Revelation, John's glimpse of Christ was here before the throne. John saw Him in human likeness, clothed with a white robe down to His feet and encircled with a golden band across His chest. His head and hair were so bright in Heaven's glory, they looked white as snow. His feet, however, appeared to gleam like burnished bronze. His eyes were like penetrating flames of fire.[13]

People in modern times also have seen Him. Lorne Fox gives this description:

> I saw the Master, bathed in the golden light of Heaven's atmosphere. He was looking at me, and there was divine love in that impelling look. I felt it surge through me.
>
> His robe: it was white and glistening, and it was studded with tiny, bright pin-pointed gems that shone like gold and silver. I saw the broad golden band around His waist; the upper part of His garments were white as snow.
>
> Then His face! How can I describe the

face of the Master? It was a strong face . . .
ageless, expressing eternity. His hair was
golden in the light that shone down upon
Him.

It is difficult to determine the actual color of His
hair, since it seems to take on a different appearance
in the various hues of Heaven's light. Fox continues:

> A smile played upon His lips . . . and in
> that moment, in His smile, I once again saw
> the pearly gates . . . heard the angels sing
> . . . and saw the streets of gold . . . and the
> mansions . . . the music of Heaven again
> was in my soul. All this, in my Master's
> smile.
> His eyes! What words of man can explain
> them? His eyes met mine, and for a moment
> His divine love emanated from them into
> mine. Then His look changed. He was
> analyzing me . . . reading me like a book.
> He saw the good things. He saw the small,
> mean things; and He looked carefully at
> them all. Then, suddenly, His eyes were
> full of love; and a glorious truth flooded my
> soul:
> In that moment, I was aware that my
> Master knew all about me . . . everything
> there was to know . . . but He loved me just
> the same.[14]

A description of Jesus must begin at the throne of
God. It was there among the great bursts of light,
flashing like diamonds in the sun, I met Him. I
remember not only the awesome dignity and
majesty of that moment, but a strange sense of

belonging and relief. "Praise the Lord, I finally made it," I thought.

Yet in the moments to come, I would be given a choice. Would I stay in His presence and take my place among the splendors of this city? Or would I accept His commission and return with a mission, which He would now reveal?

10

Countdown and Reentry

All around me the sounds of myriad choristers blended in rich and exquisite harmony. The impressions of a million tones, ranging from deep, mellow bass to voices in the highest registers, were refreshing showers of peace and joy.

Because my attention was focused on Jesus, some of the details must be painted by others. They too are frustrated by the inability to describe the splendor of that heavenly city, even with their sensory awareness heightened by the closeness to supernatural power.

The throne of God filled my consciousness with a reddish-brown and yellow glow of chalcedony, a precious quartz, surrounded by the glistening aura of emerald-green light. A majestic rainbow arched high over the throne like a massive crowning dome, and the throne seemed to extend for miles along a transparent sea of golden glass, stretching into the far distance to accommodate millions of worshiping angels and departed spirits. They continually thronged before it in convocations of praise and adoration, and the sounds of their worship reverberated throughout the city like the rumbles of mighty rolling thunder or the waves of a hundred oceans crashing on distant shores.

I am often asked the location of this majestic throne. As I was caught up from the hospital bed, I seemed to be spinning through outer space in a northerly direction.

Later, I remembered Bible references that support my experience. We are told that Satan, when desiring to be like God, declared he would exalt himself above the stars in the north.[1] The suffering Job of antiquity declared God's locale to be in the north.[2] And today, a popular Christian song from Psalm 48 tells of Mount Zion, the city of the great King, situated in the far north.[3]

As described in the Bible, this celestial throne is surrounded by seven lighted lamps, a golden altar burning with celestial fire, and twenty-four smaller thrones of sparkling beauty. One witness gazed upon a vast number of glittering, golden seats rising like the tiered terraces of a great amphitheater from the back, right and left sides of the throne. On one occasion, the witness said, a 100,000-voice choir, each chorister with a golden harp, filled the whole city with their magnificent melodies from this immense auditorium.

As exciting as the glories of this realm appear, nothing captured the feeling of Heaven like the very presence of Christ, whose rapt attention I now enjoyed.

Secrets Revealed

Realizing this was the crowning moment of my life, questions nevertheless raced from my mind to His. "Lord, I'm here in Heaven, in your presence. But what about the prophecies people have given me concerning things that are going to happen in my life?"

"I am taking care of those," came His loving reply.

"But if I stay here, I'm going to make false prophets out of those people. And what about the thirty-five years of unanswered prayer?" I persisted.

With the sensation of a warm, knowing smile, He answered, "I have control of everything. All things that happen are of my design and choosing. Even this. You are here because I want you here."

"How are you going to fulfill those prophecies?" I pressed reverently.

"It is not yet time for you to know how."

I interrogated further. "Lord, what about the last day revival some have been predicting?"

Only a part of Jesus' answer can now be revealed. The rest is sealed until the time He releases it. Until then, I cannot even discuss it with my wife.

"I have control of my church," He began, "and the power that is going to be unleashed in my church is hitherto unknown to man."

"How will this be?" I asked.

"Soon I am coming back to Earth *with* my church," Jesus explained. "But first I must come *for* it. And before I come for my church, I will come *to* it in a visitation greater than man has ever known."

Some time after this heavenly encounter, while reading my Bible one day, Jesus impressed upon me that He would complete the prophecies of Isaiah 61, including the one recorded in verse 11: ". . . The Lord will cause righteousness and praise to spring forth before all nations." To accomplish this the church will unite and denominationalism fade, a phenomenon we are now observing.

I believe the church will set the fashions of the

world, and that before He comes, the wealth of the world will be turned over to the church so that the people will look to it for subsistence."[4]

While I was with Him, Jesus pledged to restore unity and wealth to the church and to release His power that has been held back for centuries. This will be felt politically and spiritually as the forces of God and evil battle for control of planet Earth.

As He spoke, understanding flashed through my mind. God made Adam and Eve neither mortal nor immortal. He made them eternal. God said, "Let us make man in our image."[5] Adam, not Solomon, was the wisest man who ever lived. He named all the animals, all the trees, all the life forms of Earth. God said, "Adam, be fruitful . . . and replenish the earth, and subdue it: and have dominion. . . ."[6] The first couple did well until they ate of the forbidden fruit. In such rebellion, they learned of the existence of evil and lost their dominion to Satan.

Through the centuries, mankind has sought to regain control. Great empires have risen and fallen. Alexander the Great, Julius Ceasar, Napoleon, Hitler: many have been the conquerors in history. Yet the principalities of man ultimately crumbled.

Silently and militantly, meanwhile, another kingdom has risen. Coming as a babe in the manger and winning His throne on the cross, the conqueror from the world beyond, Jesus Christ, brought change to the human soul.

As many as received Him as Lord and Savior, He recreated and recruited. Called the "church," this great body of Christ's followers has risen like a massing army, marching through the centuries as valiant warriors. While empires of men rose and fell, the kingdom of God enveloped the world without end. No other king has vanquished so many, yet until now His militant forces could not use all the power vested in Adam before his fall. Within each recreated soul exists the potential of Adam's dominion and might, a power God is beginning to restore in these last days of Earth.

Accompanying the restoration of Adam's authority, I learned, is the power to heal sick bodies, to restore amputated arms or legs and to perform other creative miracles, to raise the dead and to "cause righteousness and praise to spring forth before all nations." The wisdom and stature of leadership is another phenomenon to accompany this restoration, for the church is to have a vastly greater influence in government and world affairs before the Lord returns.

With this understanding indelibly impressed upon me, my attention suddenly was diverted to a distant scene. Peering through the sea of golden glass before God's throne, I saw my body lying on its bed. The glassy sea appeared to magnify the intensive care unit of the hospital like a huge telescopic lens.

Death . . . Turn This Man Loose

The hospital appeared to have no roof, and for the first time I viewed the layout of the medical building. Hospital personnel scurried about the halls, in and out of the rooms, attending patients. Two nurses were frantically trying to revive my body, while a third was calling for a doctor—any doctor! So clear was the view I could see that my heart monitor on the wall had been unplugged.

Suddenly, my gaze shifted to a white car parked near the entrance to the hospital, and I saw a familiar person entering the building. My eyes followed Pastor Wilkerson as he walked briskly down the corridors leading to the intensive care unit. He quickly approached the closed ICU door and knocked. The nurse ushered him in, offering no resistance.

"Lord, it looks like trouble down there," I quipped, not daring to take my eyes off the unfolding drama. Intuitively, I knew the moment of decision had come as Pastor Wilkerson picked up my lifeless left hand and commanded me to return.

"Death, I rebuke you in the all-authoritative name of Jesus," he began firmly. "I command you to loose your hold, and I command his spirit to come back into his body!"

Suddenly, I felt the strong magnetic earthward tug of his prayer.

Commissioned for a Mission

"Lord, what shall I do?" I pleaded, confused at this turn of events.

"What do you want to do?" His reply flashed into my mind.

In the midst of all this glory, who would want to return to all my problems?

Earlier that New Year's Day, when Pastor Wilkerson had suddenly felt the urge to come to the hospital to pray for me, he did not know I had already died. Even upon entering the room, he was not certain about my death. There had been no pronouncement; the sheet had not been pulled over my head; the nurse was still trying to reach a doctor.

As the Pastor continued to rebuke death, I heard him quote the words of Jesus recorded in the Bible: "The thief cometh not, but for to steal, and to kill and to destroy: I am come that they might have life, and that they might have it more abundantly. I am the resurrection, and the life: he that believeth in me, though he were dead, yet shall he live."[7]

Again the tug. Only stronger.

"Lord, I don't want to leave your presence, but I died unfulfilled. I know a definite ministry awaits me there."

"Remember, I have never lost a battle, nor even a skirmish," He replied.

The prophecies again crossed my mind as I continued, "Lord, are you doing this for a specific reason?"

"Yes, my son. It will take this in your life because I have been dealing with you all these years. The burden you have had and your prayers have not been of your own making, but I have planted them in your heart. I am conditioning you for a mission."

"Lord, if I go back, will you go with me?"

"Son, I have given you my Word: 'Lo, I am with you alway, even unto the end of the world.'[8] I have never left you," He chided gently, "and I never will leave you nor forsake you."

"Yes, Lord," I returned meekly, feeling ashamed at some of the places I had taken Him. "I'll go back. But will you grant me that ministry I've longed for?"

Still watching the events below, I felt another strong pull as Pastor Wilkerson continued my recall.

"Go back, my son, with this commission," Jesus commanded. "Join forces with the rest of my army that will usher in my kingdom age. Miraculous signs will accompany your ministry."

Does this mean I'll still be alive on Earth when Jesus returns for His church? His statement cannot easily be explained, but that's what I believe.

With the quickness of a snapping finger, I wooshed through the stars and reentered my body with a jolt. It felt cold upon impact. Seeing I was alive, both the nurse and Pastor Wilkerson burst into action. As he jubilantly praised God, the excited nurse quickly plugged in the heart monitor.

Immediately the beep . . . beep . . . beeping of the machine echoed my heartbeat.

By this time, I was aware of my surroundings once more. I knew precisely what had happened to me. My physical organs were functioning again. I was excited! First, I thanked my pastor for coming. Then, I started to relate the whole story to him.

"Shh. . . ," he whispered, index finger over his lips. "Don't speak." Then he slipped away. I think I must have grinned smugly as I warmed beneath the covers. "Oh," I reasoned, "he doesn't want me to use up my new strength."

At my last glance toward the clock on the wall, the hands had read ten minutes past two, with ebony darkness engulfing the room. When I fully regained my faculties, I looked again at the clock—ten minutes until three! For at least thirty of those forty minutes, medical science and prayer had labored to retrieve me from the other side.

Three miracles had taken place: God spoke to a man, and he obeyed; life came back to my body after approximately thirty minutes of clinical death; and no brain damage occurred.

I have been told by many physicians that if the brain is deprived of oxygen for three or four minutes, serious brain damage can result, and the patient is usually left nothing more than a human vegetable. I knew everybody thought I had brain damage. I have since said over and over again that I don't know what happened to my brain, but whatever it was, I like this one better.

I remained lying there, watching the minute hand sweep the face of time—not realizing my spirit was about to peer into the future.

11

Glimpses of the Future

I lay quietly on my bed in the ICU, filling the twilight between sleep and consciousness with thoughts about the wonder of my visit to Heaven and my conversation with Jesus.

Suddenly, I was wide awake and sitting on a platform in an open square. Before me were tens of thousands of people, standing because there were no seats. I looked around at the brightly painted shops surrounding the square and focused on a beautiful old cathedral topped by vaulting spires.

How did I get there? Had I left my body again and traveled into the future in another dimension to this strange locale? Or was I still lying in bed, but having a vision? It happened so suddenly I can't remember. I know this: it was no dream.

Colombia

In some way I knew I was in Bogotá, capital of Colombia in South America, attending a massive open-air evangelistic meeting. People were jammed shoulder to shoulder, listening intently to the evangelist, who was preaching with all the feeling he could muster, without making much of an impact.

Then from the midst of the crowd came a small, brown teenage boy who stepped up on the platform near me and walked over to the microphone. He had stringy hair and strange eyes, and looked as though he had just come out of the jungle.

The crowd became electrified by a sense of the Holy Spirit's presence and power as the youth spoke. People broke down and wept. I saw thousands lift their hands in surrender to Jesus, while thousands more were baptized in the Holy Spirit.

In the crowd, I spotted a man on crudely-made crutches. He had only one leg—his left—but as I watched incredulously, the right leg appeared! In astonishment he threw the crutches high in the air and began dancing around the crowd, praising God for the miracle.

Nearby, another man prayed with only one arm raised—the only one he had. Before my eyes, by the power of God, he suddenly had two arms and was waving them about in the air. Another incredible miracle!

All among that multitude, people were being healed, spiritually reborn, and transformed by the Holy Spirit. Wheelchairs were emptied, stretchers and crutches thrown aside while this young boy spoke.

As my eyes scanned the crowd, I spotted a small group of clergymen over to one side. It was obvious from their dress that they were men of great influence in the Roman Catholic Church in Colombia. As they talked among themselves, one exclaimed, "This is just an ignorant boy! He is not one of us, and he is not one of them [meaning a Protestant]. He must come directly from God!"

183

At this they all began to weep and pray, praising God for His goodness. It was clear that a great spiritual awakening was beginning that would sweep the whole continent, reaching Protestants and Catholics alike.

This was the first of eight such experiences the Lord gave me as I lay on my hospital bed during those early days of January 1972. Before then, I was as skeptical of visions as I was of personal prophecies. Isn't it amazing how dying, going to be with Jesus, and returning to Earth can change one's perspective? To me, the supernatural had become just as normal as the natural world.

I can't explain how these visions took place; I don't know. I read in the Bible that Paul was caught up into the third heaven, but even he could not say whether he was in or out of his body.[1] It was the same with me. All I can do is tell you what was revealed to me. I cannot answer how or why.

I *do* know, however, that it was not levitation or any other occult experience. I was taken by the Holy Spirit in His own sovereign will, not mine. Occult experiences come to persons who seek information and powers that have been veiled and forbidden by God.[2] I did not seek the visions, but rather was shown the truth of things to come as a gift of revelation.[3]

In the end, visions must always be tested, just as prophecies are, to determine their validity according to the principles of God's revealed Word, the Bible, and whether they come to pass.

I have not yet seen this first vision fulfilled, but only a partial confirmation of its fulfillment, much as with the other seven visions.

This verification came about two years later, when Olive was telling this story to Cliff Dudley,

184

then president of Creation House publishers, at a Full Gospel Business Men's meeting in Riverside, California. As she told of the young boy and his impact on the people, Cliff began rubbing his arms in excitement.

"Wow!" he exclaimed. "My goose bumps are having goose bumps. I know who that young man is!"

He explained that his company was soon to publish a book about a missionary to the Motilone Indians of Colombia.[4] In preparing the book, Cliff had been to Colombia and had met this boy, a young man who travels from village to village, preaching the gospel in languages he has not learned.

"The reason he looked different," Cliff explained, "is that Orientals married into that Indian tribe centuries ago, and the people have retained Oriental eyes and features.

"Marvin," he asked, as I joined the conversation, "would you recognize this boy if I sent you his picture?"

"Absolutely," I replied excitedly. "I don't know a Motilone from a Navajo, but I could never forget his face."

"I'll send you one of the first books off the press," Cliff said enthusiastically. "He's in a group photo somewhere. See if you can find him."

A few weeks later, the book arrived. I thumbed through it nervously, looking carefully at all the pictures, until one particular face seemed to jump off the page! Sure enough, it was him. There could be no mistake.

Later, I learned that my young evangelist was Odo Moto, an orphan who had been adopted by Bobarishora, the first Christian convert of the Motilone tribe. Inspired by the Holy Spirit, he was just beginning an unusual ministry among tribes that are virtually unknown to outsiders, preaching to them in their own languages by the spiritual gift of tongues.[5] A great spiritual awakening is just beginning in South America, and I fully expect Odo Moto to play a major part in it.

A confirmation has also come regarding the miraculous creation of arms and legs I saw. In February 1977, I was describing my vision of Bogotá to an audience in Santa Barbara, California. After the service, a family who had just come from Colombia ran up to me excitedly.

"Señor Ford," one of them exclaimed, "this has already begun to happen in my country. Just a few weeks ago, a man in Bogotá whose arm had been amputated was given a new, healthy arm by God's power!"

During the same vision of South America, God showed me something else, which was confirmed completely in 1974. I believe He showed me this to reassure me that all the other visions, too, would come to pass.

This time I saw myself ministering in a small village in Peru. I remember noticing a badly damaged cathedral, leaning precariously with twisted spires. Nearby was a funeral procession.

In October 1974, I actually went to Peru and worked with Rev. Hobart Vann, a Southern Baptist minister, and three other pastors. We cooperated with the Wycliffe Bible Translators and ministered to Indian tribes and people in the cities, both Catholic and Protestant.

On our tour, we reached the little town of Chincha Alta and were driving our station wagon through the town when I drew up in sudden amazement. I stared open-mouthed at the exact cathedral I had seen in my vision almost three years earlier.

With chills going up my spine, I described the miracle to those who were with me and concluded by mentioning that the only thing missing was the funeral procession. I recalled that at the end of the procession there was an old Ford van, covered with flowers and carrying a large cross of red and white flowers at its rear.

Just as the words left my mouth, we turned the corner. And there it was! A long procession of mourners was walking slowly down the street, carrying a flower-bedecked casket. At the end came the van, covered with flowers. We watched in shaking excitement as the van passed our location, carrying a large cross of red and white carnations!

After that, I would never again doubt the validity of the visions the Lord had given me in that hospital room. They have not all come to pass yet, but I know they will.

India

In my next vision, God took me to India, where I found myself with an evangelistic team, ministering to people in a large rural area. The platform was lit by the harsh glow of a string of bare electric bulbs, and a primitive amplification system allowed us to speak to the thousands of people crushing toward the front.

I sensed the cresting of a great spiritual awakening in India. There had been persecution, I felt, but it was evaporating as hundreds of thousands turned to Christ.

I watched as customs began to change. The starvation-wracked country became more prosperous. Wells were dug, crops came in abundantly, poverty declined. People were being born again and healed *en masse*.

187

East Africa

I was taken next to East Africa—once more to a rural area near a large city. The area was hilly and dry, with few trees to give shelter from the afternoon heat. The people—most of them bare from the waist up—had walked for days from their villages to come to our meeting, which lasted for the better part of a week.

This time we had no lights and no sound system—just a team of us preaching the gospel to the thousands who were eagerly gathered. Some of the time I had an interpreter, but other times I did not. Whether they were English-speaking or God was miraculously providing the interpretation, I didn't know.

Our team, working with local Christians, ministered to the needs of the people, but the crowd was much too large to reach individually. I remember waving my hand over the audience and seeing thousands healed at once, including such miracles as the creating of missing limbs. As people met Jesus, they returned to their villages and joyfully told what had happened. As in India, the land began to prosper.

Before I was taken from Africa, God showed me the whole continent turning to Christ. In South Africa there were mass evangelistic meetings in stadiums and open fields. In northwest Africa, they prayed for rain to relieve severe drought, and the rains came. People were jumping around happily in the downpour, shouting and praising God. The Christian growth we are seeing in Africa today is only the beginning of what God showed me in this vision.

The Orient

From Africa I was taken to the Orient. Part of this vision I have seen fulfilled, especially in Taiwan. God showed me He would sweep the Far East, starting in Korea and Taiwan, then moving to Japan and even Red China.

In the vision I saw evangelistic teams preaching, singing, and healing the sick. In one meeting, a whole section of blind people simultaneously received their sight. Groups of deaf-mutes could suddenly hear and praise God aloud. Mass meetings were followed by solid instruction in the churches, as Christianity spread like wildfire through the Orient.

I saw God's power of spiritual renewal moving through Red China, beginning with small groups. Communists came to heckle meetings, making so much noise we had to shout to be heard. A few Christians were arrested, but God forced their release and bound the hecklers so they could not move or speak. Opposition melted before the superior power of Jesus Christ.

God showed me a large stadium in Taiwan where thousands of people were mobbing the platform, hungry for God. I saw mass healings and conversions. I knew this would open a great ministry on that island.

In August 1974, I stood in that very stadium as part of an evangelistic crusade led by the popular Chinese evangelist, Nora Lam. The location was Kaohsiung, Taiwan's second largest city.

Exactly as I had seen from my hospital bed, people were pressed together with hands raised, praising God. They were being brought up to the platform for healing, and we laid hands on them and prayed for four or five at a time.

Just as in my vision, I saw hundreds being healed. Eventually we had to spread out through that teeming crowd to reach many others in need. By the end of the meeting, more than ten thousand persons had signed cards declaring a decision for Christ. There would have been even more if we hadn't run out of cards!

Monday, August 5, we stayed in our hotel room all day to fast and pray. That night a man in the crowd was sitting in a wheelchair. They told me he had been paralyzed in a sitting position for more than two years. Through the interpreter, I told him to expect God to heal him as I laid my hands on him.

I put my hands on his head, said a simple prayer and stood back. Raising my arm to point at him, I commanded, "In the name of Jesus Christ, stand up and walk!"

I took his hand as he stood up shakily and walked halfway across the stadium floor and back. We soon had to return him to the wheelchair because of his weakened condition, but he has since gained strength and is still walking to this day.

At the same meeting, a captain of the Kaohsiung police force hobbled up on crutches to Olive. He had broken a leg and crushed his foot in a motorcycle accident. He wanted prayer for healing.

Olive looked frantically around the huge crowd for me, but I wasn't in sight. "Marvin can't heal him anyway," she reasoned. She knelt at his feet (it being considered degrading for a woman to touch a Chinese man's head), grasped his ankles and prayed. The officer disappeared into the crowd, still on his crutches.

A short time later, when we were at the Taipei airport preparing to return home, the tall Manchurian captain came running up to us, grinning. His name, we learned, was Paul Chen. He told us that he had been completely healed and no longer needed his daily dose of expensive pain pills.

"Yesterday," said Captain Chen dramatically, "like this." He limped across the floor. "Today, like this!" He walked normally, stomping his formerly crushed foot to show us it was wholly healed.

He took off his shoe and tapped his foot. "See? See?" he beamed. "Yesterday, Buddhist. Today, Christian!"

As we walked to our plane, he followed us as far as he could, shaking hands all around, with tears rolling down his face.

Israel

My fifth vision was of Israel. Here, evangelism was more on a one-to-one basis, rather than the mass meetings of the other visions. As people accepted Jesus as Messiah, they would go out joyfully and tell their friends; then they would meet together to report their success. Resistance was encountered from the rabbis, but the movement was spreading so fast, nothing could stop it. The long-promised awakening of the Jews is just around the corner.[6]

Europe

From Israel I was carried to Europe. I saw crowded meetings everywhere, mostly in big stadiums. Like the other continents, the European renewal was characterized by healings, spiritual rebirths, and baptisms in the Holy Spirit as evangelistic teams stirred the dying embers of Christianity.

United States

Then I was brought back to the United States and

shown how He planned to use me here. I saw myself in homes and in large auditoriums, ministering to people as I had longed to do for thirty-five years. I was teaching those who already were active in ministry how to submit to the Holy Spirit and release His power within them. I exercised the spiritual gift known as the "word of knowledge"—selecting people in an audience as God gives the knowledge and revealing their particular need. And people were being healed of many diseases as God performed miracles spontaneously without my having to touch them.

Already this ministry has begun as I travel around the United States. Don't think I'm complacent about these powers of the Holy Spirit. I am still in awe every time God decides to use me this way. In fact, I was downright scared the first time such power was manifested.

It was in 1974, during a Full Gospel Business Men's breakfast in Concord, California. I told the standing audience that God was going to heal all there, and as I began to wave my hand over the crowd, about fifteen of them fell to the floor, divine energy surging through their bodies.

I can't explain this phenomenon. I had nothing to do with it. But such spectacular demonstrations of God's touch have occurred many times since. In tiny Dows, Iowa, it was especially strong one evening in 1975 as we held meetings at the United Methodist church. I was praying for the sick on the platform when I became aware of a loud "thump-thump" out in the audience. Looking up in curiosity, I saw people in the congregation falling down in rows like dominoes. Some fell on seats, some between seats, others in the aisles, as if they had all suddenly fainted. Before it was over, more than three-fourths of the 230 people in attendance had been felled by the Holy Spirit. And no one was hurt. It was as if invisible hands had eased their fall.

I really don't know why God does this, but it is undeniable that He does. The phenomenon accompanied Kathryn Kuhlman, and it is common during miracle services at Melodyland and in the ministries of many ordinary people like myself. It is not emotionalism; usually no emotion is associated with it. Someone just quietly falls, often without even being touched. The phenomenon is no guarantee of healing, nor a spiritual barometer; it happens to Christians and non-Christians alike and has occurred from Bible days down through the history of the church.[7] And it was common among some of the early evangelists of modern times. My only explanation is that when omnipotence touches mortal flesh, something has to give!

Government Officials

In the eighth and final vision God gave me during those days in the hospital, I was shown how He will move among government officials all over the world, so they will endorse evangelism among their people. Although the complete fulfillment is yet to come, we have begun to see this happen in Taiwan, Korea, and Hawaii.

Finally, after three days of such rapture, my visions ended. I have had only a few since, but I am absolutely convinced that what I saw was shown to me by God Himself—for His own purposes.

A few days after the last vision, on January 9, I was moved out of intensive care and into a regular hospital ward. God began my new life of ministry—the life for which I had prayed so earnestly—almost immediately.

People came to visit and pray for me. Instead, I would suddenly get messages from God for them! I had never done this before.

It began with a woman who had predicted my coming ministry two years previously. Now I had a prophecy for her, which concerned her ministry in Baja, California.

Later, a minister came to visit, and the Lord showed me he had been living in sin for many years. If he would obey God, I was led to tell him, his ministry would flourish.

Even Maria, the nurse who had been with me all through the heart attack, received a message from the Lord. She had been praying for a baby, and I heard myself tell her that in a year's time she would be pregnant. And a year later, she was!

It got so that people were nearly standing in line to come into my room. Olive was becoming worried because I was talking constantly, yet she knew something miraculous had happened to me. After all those years of frustration, I had finally been brought to the point where God wanted me, and He began using me in service to others.

But what about those visions? Were they real, or just hallucinations induced by morphine? And what about the prophecies? Were they just lucky guesses? Would God really do all this for an ordinary person like me?

12

Visions Come True

Visions of the sort I had are not new; the Bible is full of them. Abraham was shown his descendants as stars of the sky.[1] Moses saw the Promised Land before he died.[2] The prophet Ezekiel was transported by the Holy Spirit to the gate of the temple.[3]

Saint Peter was shown his coming mission to the Gentiles,[4] as was the Apostle Paul his call to Macedonia.[5] Stephen, the martyr, saw into Heaven,[6] and John, the author of the Book of Revelation, not only caught a glimpse of Heaven, but of the Earth's future.[7]

Visions are views of realities given supernaturally. They are not hallucinations or products of the subconscious mind. Nor are they dreams, for the person is wide awake. In both the Old and New Testaments, visions were considered authoritative and reliable. If God gave them in the past, can He not do so today? This phenomenon was predicted for the last days and has been experienced throughout the church age.[8]

While the Bible is the only infallible Word of God,

His revelations to man are progressive. Visions, prophecies, or any other supernatural gift cannot be accepted as the Bible is, but an undeniable fact remains that today God is revealing more and more of the world beyond. Jesus said the Holy Spirit would reveal "things to come."[9] Visions are, in part, the means by which He reveals them.

Not all visions come from God. Much of what people claim to have seen is nothing more than hallucination induced by too much mince pie or an overactive imagination. In some cases the phenomenon has been satanic.

One tells the difference by applying these tests:

First, *does it harmonize with biblical teaching*—in both principle and statement? Or does it undermine God's authority?

Second, *how does the vision influence the individual*? Are God's laws of life disregarded? Does one's experience leave the one rational or deluded?

Third, *does the vision uplift the name of Jesus*? Evil spirits can give people visions, but they will never confess that Jesus is God come in the flesh. This is the ultimate test. Any element of a vision that does not uphold this confession is clue enough to its origin.

Fourth, *do the visions come to pass as promised*?

Beyond their harmony with the Bible, the visions and prophecies I have received certainly honor and glorify Jesus, for each is concerned with bringing people to Him as Lord and Savior. What I saw was a continuation of His ministry while on Earth, and that is exactly what He promised.[10] Worldwide renewal by the power of Christ is what the Bible predicts[11] and also what God has independently revealed in recent times to thousands of His people, all dedicated to the Lord and His truth. The authenticity of these revelations is supported by the similarities and agreement among the predictions—and their fulfillment.

Fulfillment Has Begun

What I saw is now in the process of being fulfilled. My ministry has begun to flourish as God promised. It started in my hospital bed and is spreading around the globe.

Visions of the funeral in Peru and the stadium crusade in Taiwan have been completely fulfilled. Others, such as the boy in Colombia, give every indication of coming fulfillment. God will complete the works He has shown me, just as He honored the call and promises He made regarding my ministry so many years ago. In the years since my journey to the other side, God has taken me around the world in His service, on hundreds of speaking engagements each year.

Beginning in the spring of 1972, when I first told about leaving my body, God has been using me to bring teaching, healing, salvation, the ministries of the Holy Spirit, and deliverance from the fear of death to many thousands of people. Following trips to Taiwan, Colombia, Peru, and Bolivia, we were called to Guatemala and East Africa, where we worked with missionaries.

We briefly visited the Holy Land, then began an intensive ministry all over the United States during 1976. That same year I was interviewed by Pat Robertson on the Christian Broadcasting Network, and the story of my death and return was published in the Full Gospel Business Men's magazine, *Voice*. My story also has been related by Ralph Wilkerson in his book *Beyond and Back*, a book about people who have died and lived to tell it.

To keep our scheduling straight, Olive was forced to convert our dining room into an office, complete with desk, electric typewriter, and filing cabinets—to say nothing of the materials she needs as a musician and composer.

The year 1977 was even more intense. We began alternating between single appearances and three to five day seminars we call "Life in the Spirit." In just one part of that year, our single engagements totaled forty in thirty-six days, plus radio and television broadcasts. We spent part of the summer ministering in Japan and in Hawaii, where I talked at length with the lieutenant governor. On our return, we spent the remainder of the year in meetings from coast to coast in the United States and Canada. As of this writing we are looking forward to a trip to India as the Lord leads me more and more into the worldwide ministry He promised.

In the midst of all this activity, I often think back to those days of failure and agonizing prayer, to my crushing loss of hope in the hospital and to the day when Dr. Rutherford had said to me, "Marvin, I guess you don't know it, but you're retired. If you ever get an okay to return to work, it certainly won't be from me."

I am awed by the love and miraculous power of Christ in raising me from death and using this poor, shy boy from Waco to help evangelize the world. We have never looked for large crowds nor tried to follow the pattern of big-name evangelists. We have simply shared Jesus and what He has done for us, confident that all our needs will be met.

As a result, we have reached the poor and the rich, the failures and the successes, those on skid row and on yachts, with the message of Jesus' love. Our travels have taken us to every type of congregation, from Pentecostal to mainline Protestant to Catholic, and all have responded to God's power. There has not been one service where God has not healed, saved, or baptized people in His Spirit.

The physical healings are the most dramatic part of the meetings, and I'm seeing more and more miracles take place. The need is so great, I can no longer always pray with individuals. Instead, I often ask my audiences to clasp one another's hands as I pray, and God helps them where they are. This way, no one gets any glory but Jesus.

I remember a young man in Honolulu who was severely addicted to drugs, one of many we have encountered in our services. He was suffering withdrawal pain when we prayed for him, and God instantly delivered him from the addiction. God showed me He was calling this boy into the ministry, and I told him so. This confirmed what God had already revealed to him, and he leaped off the high platform with a shout of joy.

In La Paz, capital of Bolivia, we met a prostitute in her late teens. She was an epileptic, but in repeated counseling sessions with her Catholic priest, it had become apparent that something more was wrong. At the close of one of our services there, she came forward for prayer. I sensed she was possessed by an evil spirit, and I commanded it to come out of her by the authority of Jesus' name.

The girl fell to the floor, writhing in agony as her deliverance began. From her mouth poured a flood of curses and obscenities, greatly embarrassing the priest who was our host. Together we knelt down and gently laid hands on her small, frail form. As we prayed, her tormentor was exorcized with jerking hiccup sounds. Soon her eyes became bright and her face calm; we knew she was delivered.

We were in Guatemala City one Saturday evening six months later for a youth musical program. Señor Munoz, the leader of the rally, asked me to pray for a young man whose leg had been broken in a drunk driving accident. The doctors had inserted two pins into the bone, but the leg would not heal. In agony, he hobbled around on crutches.

Later that night, after we had prayed for him, his Christian wife said to him, "Why don't you quit using your crutches? That man prayed for your healing, didn't he?"

Despite his pain, he decided to trust God. Gingerly, he laid the crutches aside and discovered to his surprise that he could walk. The pain left, and he began to run happily up and down the stairs. We saw him the next day as he marched triumphantly into church, carrying the crutches over his shoulder like a rifle. He had not only been healed, but had surrendered his life to Christ.

In the fall of 1975, we ministered in Kenya, East Africa, with several missionaries. One of them, Art Dodzweit, was suffering acute back pain but told none of us about it. During one of the church services, I sensed that someone in the congregation was being healed of back pain, and I asked whomever it was to come forward. Bounding happily to the front, Art said he had been scheduled for back surgery, but the pain was now completely gone.

Olive experienced a similar healing a few days afterward when we were in Mombasa. Because of a childhood fall, she had grown up with a drastic curvature of the spine, accompanied by severe, intermittent pain. On this particular Sunday, Holy Communion was being served from the "common cup." She put aside her fear of drinking from the cup and drank in honor of the Lord. "Father," she prayed, "I partake of this cup—not as one of disease, but as one of health." As she did, her back pain faded away.

In 1977, we held meetings in Tenryu-City, Japan, and during our stay met a young man at the missionary home of our host, George Bostrom. He had been crippled in hand and foot since childhood and had been born deaf, capable of making only repulsive, harsh sounds. He came by the home often to ridicule the "big" Americans, whose features seemed grotesque to him.

One day, I felt I should pray for his healing. As I prayed, something popped in his ears and he began to shriek with glee. Jumping up, he ran over to the organ with a sort of hopping gait, and gestured frantically for Olive to play it. As she struck chord after chord, he was beside himself with happiness, hearing music for the first time.

Now he must learn to speak. His hand and foot were not restored, but the congregation is still praying for that. Only God knows why healings are sometimes incomplete, but in His time all things will be accomplished. Everyone in that town knows of this deaf boy, and the miracle he experienced will surely be used to open their minds and hearts to the reality of a resurrected Christ.

On that same trip to Japan, a middle-aged man was brought to me for prayer. A stroke had left his right side and vocal chords paralyzed for five years. I spoke a simple prayer of faith, then asked him to say "Jesus." Haltingly, he made the attempt. His face brightened in amazement at the sound of his own voice. Healed, he grabbed me excitedly with his formerly paralyzed hand and squeezed till my arm hurt.

One evening, my wife and I were at the home of

Steve Allen, the television host and comedian, where Olive was to accompany a group of singers at a large gathering. One of the women crowding around the swimming pool tripped on a concrete ridge circling the water and fell to the hard patio surface.

We lifted her gently onto a chaise lounge, and as she lay there groaning in pain, I received a distinct impression from the Lord.

"Her knee is broken. Pray for her."

"Right here?" I thought, looking around at all those sophisticated people.

"Right here," came the inward response. "You don't have to make a scene."

As I prayed, a Jewish girl who had accepted Jesus as Messiah knelt down and joined me. Soon the woman's pain began to fade. Someone had gone for a pain pill, but the girl said pleadingly, "Don't take it. God wants to heal you."

About then the girl's father, a doctor, was summoned and began to examine the rapidly swelling knee.

"She has a broken a kneecap," I said.

The doctor looked at me suspiciously. "How do *you* know what's wrong with her?"

"I just know. That's all I can say," I replied lamely.

Scowling, the doctor made a brief examination, then turned back to me in amazement. "It is broken," he gasped. Turning his attention to the woman, he offered her a pain pill.

"I don't need it now," she beamed. "The pain is nearly gone." They drove her to the hospital, but by the time they arrived, the bones had knitted together. Her healing was confirmed. I am always amazed that God is ready at any time to answer a prayer of faith, whether in Hollywood or East Africa.

And He takes care of His own. Suffering intense pain in her back for ten years after an automobile accident, Jean Friesen, a preacher's wife, came to one of our meetings in Albert Lea, Minnesota. Looking around the crowd in that packed YMCA auditorium, I sensed someone was present with a severe back problem. I asked the person, whoever he or she was, to come forward. The woman hesitantly walked to the front, and I prayed for her. Knowing inwardly that she had been healed, I told her to bend over and touch the floor. Her faith stimulated, she extended both arms all the way down.

"God has healed me!" she exclaimed. "Before this, I even had to roll out of bed on my knees just to get up in the morning!" Her back remains healed to this day, and she is giving God the praise.

At a Full Gospel Business Men's meeting in California, Millee Pyburn was brought forward for prayer. Nearly blind at birth, scarlet fever had left her totally blind in her left eye since infancy. We prayed, and she fell to the floor under the power of God, just as so many others had. When she got up, she could see perfectly. And she still can.

Once I was called to the La Habra Community Hospital, where I had died and come back, to pray for a woman named Carole Bramel, suffering from kidney stones. Following that prayer, her thirst became unquenchable. She began to drink water incessantly until the stones were flushed out of her body with very little discomfort. The doctor sent her home, saying he needed the bed for sick people.

During a recent service at Melodyland, James Issacs, a musician from Cerritos, California, came for prayer. He had a swollen, runny sore at the back of his neck, which had been diagnosed as a virtually untreatable form of cancer. We prayed, and within three or four days, the sore was completely gone. Issacs' healing was confirmed in a written statement from his doctor.[12]

A psychologist at a mental institution, an admitted agnostic, came to our meeting in Clarksburg, West Virginia. She suffered from a muscular disease that doctors said was inoperable and incurable. I called her to the front and told the congregation she was experiencing pain in her hip and feet. She confirmed this in amazement, for she had told no one.

"Do you know Jesus Christ as your Lord and Savior?" I asked.

"Well, I thought I was a Christian once before," she replied, with tears flowing down her cheeks, "but now I know this is real."

"Then in the name of Jesus, receive your healing!" I commanded.

Instantly, she was born again and healed. She began to laugh uncontrollably as the joy of the Holy Spirit filled her. No longer an agnostic, the woman left that meeting whole in mind, body and spirit.

And so it goes, as God uses me to touch people and release them from tumors, blindness, crippled limbs, painful injuries, and incurable diseases. This is not psychic healing, as some occultists practice; it is God who does the healing. It is His demonstration of love and concern for our well-being.

Beyond the physical healings, many people wonder about this gift of the Holy Spirit called the *word of knowledge.* How do I know what ailment a person has or what his need is?

Phenomenon Explained

The word of knowledge is one of the nine supernatural gifts of the Holy Spirit listed in the Bible for use by God's people.[13] The phenomenon is a specific revelation by God to a person concerning another's needs, activities, future, or anything else of importance.

God has infinite knowledge. He knows everything that goes on. And sometimes He shares a minute portion of this knowledge with us to meet a particular need. The "word" is a witness of God's presence and is given as comfort to a person who needs the assurance that God is aware of his problem. Often it is a means of moving an individual to action when God has already been speaking to him. One uses this spiritual gift to help focus prayer on a specific need, to stimulate a person's faith or, in rare cases, to expose sin.

Many instances of the word of knowledge are recorded in the Bible. Nathan the prophet exposed David's secret murder of Uriah the Hittite and the taking of his wife, Bathsheba.[14] God told Peter of the secret sin of Ananias and Sapphira.[15]

Jesus, too, was given the word of knowledge, as when He told Peter where to find fish,[16] revealed the sordid history of the Samaritan woman,[17] and told His disciples how they would locate the room for the Last Supper.[18]

Today, the Holy Spirit grants this same gift to the church as an aid to ministry. Often, God gives me a distinct mental impression regarding someone, and in faith I reveal what He has shown me. The authenticity of this gift is demonstrated each time in its accuracy.

I recall one of the earliest times this gift was manifested. Soon after my recovery from the cardiac arrest, I was singing in the choir at Kathryn

Kuhlman's meetings in Los Angeles. The word of knowledge was a hallmark of her ministry. She would call out the healings that were taking place among the people in the audience, then ask them to come forward and give testimony. One Sunday afternoon as she did this, I realized I was receiving the impressions just before she announced them.

Often, I would turn to one of the singers next to me and say, "She's going to call out a cancer healing in that section of the auditorium," or "Right over there someone is being healed of deafness." Sure enough, that's exactly what happened. I didn't ask God for this manifestation. Today I am simply a channel through which it and other gifts may flow at His discretion.

Soon after, I was used in this gift in a public meeting in Tulare, California. The leader, Maryiann Sitton of Shiloh Retreat in Montana, surprised me with the statement, "Marvin, you have a 'word' from the Lord for someone here. Would you please come to the podium?"

Olive and I looked at each other with puzzled expressions. I didn't have a thing to say, but in faith went forward anyway. Just before I reached the front, God gave me the message. I announced that someone had just received a very disturbing letter. "In fact," I continued, "you have the letter with you now. Come forward, and the Lord will take care of the problem."

I also knew what the problem was, but didn't want to embarrass the woman who was coming forward just then, tears running down her face. Privately, I told her that the letter was from her daughter who had an illegitimate pregnancy. This the woman quietly confirmed.

"The child will be aborted through a natural

miscarriage," I said, "and your daughter will become a Christian through the experience."

In the midst of her grief, the woman found hope. God had revealed His solution to her problem.

The Human Element

The Lord is interested in our needs and sometimes gives us a message of comfort. But all such revelations should be tested, for the human element still exists in them. Caution needs to be exercised.

When a supposed "word" is not tested, or when it is sought out as a means of peering into the unknown, there is danger of error and satanic deception. I believe people have a latent sixth sense (ESP—extrasensory perception), probably a remnant of the powerful mind Adam had before his fall. Sometimes this ability is similar to the word of knowledge, and often it becomes an occult counterfeit to this word from the Lord. A person who actively solicits demonstrations of such powers becomes vulnerable to deceptions. Because of this, we are specifically told in the Bible not to seek such knowledge.[19]

If God chooses to reveal things for His own purposes, we should respond gratefully in faith. But it is quite another thing to seek information from the spiritual dimension. We are ignorant of most things in that realm; the Bible reveals only what we need for the life of faith in *this* world. When we go beyond this record, we are as infants reaching out in a strange and dangerous environment. We can easily fall prey to things we don't understand and can't properly evaluate.

Mary-Ann Brod and her husband Michael, whom I've mentioned earlier, know about this firsthand. They sought God through various occult practices.

207

"People who seek experience for experience's sake," she says, "open themselves up to whatever comes along."[20]

They began their quest for spiritual reality by getting knowledge through a Ouija board, but soon became pawns of a demon who performed miracles for them in a supposed fight against evil.

"It's an exciting thing," Mary-Ann says, "because you feel you are gaining access to knowledge that is going to free you, or that you will find what you have been searching for in your heart. But much of this is pride and leads one to be less cautious and less humble in terms of asking God about it."

She and Michael learned the hard way that supernatural knowledge is not something available on demand. Fortunately, they have been delivered from the occult bondage they endured and are serving Christ today.

Asking a minister of God for "a word from the Lord" is dangerous also, because the focus is on the word and the person giving it, not on Jesus. The Holy Spirit is not subject to man—He comes and goes as He desires. If you are receiving messages on call, whether through a Ouija board or a person who claims to be a gifted Christian, you can be sure it is not from God.

For this reason, I make certain that the focus is on Christ during all my meetings. God has gifted me with the ability to reveal divine knowledge, but I never allow people to request a "word" for themselves. God must be the one to initiate it.

For example, a man came to me after a meeting one night in northern California and said, "The Lord told me you have a word for me."

"Yes, I guess I do," I answered pleasantly. "The message is, you're not studying the Word of God enough. You're depending too much on man's word and ignoring the Bible. And His Word is a lot more important than mine."

"That's what I thought you'd say," he replied, blushing.

At another meeting in Illinois, a woman began with the same opening.

I replied, "If the Lord said I had a word for you, don't you think He'd let me in on it? Right now, He hasn't. But stick around. If the Lord gives it to me, I'll let you know."

After everyone had left the meeting, she was still waiting for that message. I told her to get the tape of my sermon.

"I've already given you three 'words' in my sermon," I said. "If God is really speaking to you, you'll find them."

The great need of the church today is for people to study the Bible and pray for understanding so they may grow into mature Christians. The word of knowledge is reserved for special circumstances.

The Lord often does give me messages for individuals. But people who constantly seek them are opening themselves to other problems. If they do get a "word," are they prepared to handle it? Will they rush off to accomplish God's promise on their own, without awaiting His time?

When God gives a message or performs a miracle, it is unmistakable. There is such a power and sweetness in it that only God can receive the glory. One incident stands out in my mind as an example.

We were ministering in the Chicago area when a mother brought in her son in a wheelchair. Part of his brain had been destroyed in Vietnam, and he was little more than a vegetable. He wore a bandage over his head with a special helmet to prevent further damage.

As I prayed for his healing, we both felt a tingling energy go through him. Pointing to his head with uncoordinated jerks, he indicated to his mother that something had taken place inside his brain. "It clicked! It clicked!" he cried feebly.

Nearly two years later, we were in Valparaiso, Indiana, when that same mother came running up to us in excitement. We stood amazed as she told us how her son, John Tomczk, is being healed. The doctors have taken bone from his ribs to cover the opening in his skull, and he is now a student at Valparaiso University, needing only a cane with which to walk. "And pretty soon," she declared, radiating with faith, "he won't even need that!"

Repeated almost daily in our ministry, such true miracles show that Jesus is alive and that He still fulfills His promises. From a hopeless failure to a corpse to a minister moving in God's power, I have been given a worldwide ministry, just as predicted. I cannot possibly doubt the prophecies and visions given to me. I see them being fulfilled every day.

Our story continues, like a 29th chapter of the Book of Acts. God has shown me other things to come, which I cannot yet reveal. Greater miracles are ahead. We have just begun to experience what the Lord had promised before the end comes.[21] I believe we are now only in the embryonic stage of the greatest spiritual revolution and restoration the world has ever seen.

Jesus said, "This gospel of the kingdom shall be preached in all the world for a witness unto all nations; and then shall the end come."[22] And throughout the Americas, India, Africa, Asia, the Middle East and Europe, I saw it happen from my hospital bed.

13

Did I Really Die?

For several days after my return from the other side, a dazzling bluish white light flooded my hospital room. It was painful to my physical eyes, and I kept them covered as much as possible with my hands.

Whether I looked up, down, to the left or to the right, there it was, intense and penetrating.[1] During this time, I was shown what God plans to do on Earth before His coming.

I have not told all that Jesus revealed during my visit beyond. The day will come when all can be disclosed, but until it is His time, my lips must remain sealed. I can say this: commissioned to help reach the world for Christ, I expect to be alive when He comes back to Earth!

When I told this to Ralph Wilkerson one day, he was startled.

"You've never been an evangelist, Marvin. How can you, a carpenter, reach the world?" Before I could reply, however, the Lord spoke the answer into Ralph's mind, so near was His presence in my room.

"I was a carpenter, and I reached the world," came the inner voice.

Others have journeyed to the other side and returned without seeing exactly what I did. What makes *me* so special?

Nothing.

And that's the reason why God is using me. All I have to do is tell people what He has done for me and leave the rest to Him.

As I tell my story, people often wonder whether I really died. Hospital officials believed I was dead.

The head nurse, who had so forcefully tried to prevent Pastor Wilkerson from seeing me in the intensive care unit, spent her break time talking with me every day during my recovery.

I was curious enough to ask why.

"I just want to come in and see what a 'dead' man talks like," she smiled.

"What do you mean?" I was puzzled. It was the first time anyone had mentioned my death.

"Well, you know . . . we lost you."

"Yes, I know. I had quite an experience."

"What happened?" She leaned forward in her chair eagerly.

"The staff was doing a fine job trying to save me," I began, "but I was in the presence of the Lord while all that was going on." I then described my experiences, and she admitted seeing a difference in me.

As we discussed my death, the nurse used the term "cardiac arrest." She confirmed that I had been dead—at least clinically—and was fascinated by what I told her.

Another evidence of my death comes from Dr. Harry I. Riegel, the cardiologist. He had given me an intensive psychological examination to see if I had the brain damage expected.

"Mr. Ford, you are a very, very lucky man," he told me.

"In what way, doc?" I feigned innocence.

"You could very well be in the cemetery right now."

I grinned weakly, not letting on that I already knew that. He began to explain my attack, describing it as a myocardial infarction. "We lost you," he concluded.

Soon after my release from the hospital, I had my first discussion on the subject with Dr. Rutherford.

"I heard you lost me in intensive care," I said casually in his office.

His eyebrows raised slightly. "Yes, that's true. It was a cardiac arrest."

"I went to be with the Lord," I told him, "and He sent me back."

As I described my experience, tears filled my doctor's eyes.

During one of my monthly visits to Dr. Morton Kritzer, who represented the insurance company, I had a chance to read Dr. Rutherford's report. It described the cardiac arrest. Based on his report and that of two other doctors, I was recommended for a hundred percent disability. I was officially retired from that moment on, but what a glorious retirement it has been!

Were it not for the miraculous intervention of prayer and the sovereign will of God, I would still be on the other side. Even if I could have been brought back by mechanical devices, as many have, I would now be a human vegetable, for the brain cannot survive more than three or four minutes without oxygen and remain undamaged.

The Final Proof

A final evidence of the reality of my experience is the change in my life and outlook. Just as Jesus' disciples were changed from cowards to men because of His resurrection, so my life has been transformed from failure to success.

In *Beyond and Back* Pastor Wilkerson identifies the important changes that take place in a Christian's life after an out-of-the-body experience. He has thoroughly investigated many such cases and personally participated in several, including mine. He says:

> A fascinating and inspiring pattern of personality changes has emerged from the experiences of Christians who have been beyond and back.
>
> Many have testified to losing their fear of death. Some, like Marvin Ford, have become more practical and life-related in their day-to-day activities. Others acknowledge losing racial prejudice and finding a new love for all people. A greater ability to understand God's Word has been reported by others.
>
> At least nine basic psychological and spiritual patterns have emerged from these case histories: life in proper focus, family priorities in correct perspective, materialism no longer an obsession, a greater sensitivity to the Holy Spirit, a spirit of revelation, a global vision, no fear of death, a more mellow nature and a new sense of joy.[2]

These changes have occurred in my life as well.

People tell me my teaching reflects a new sense of values. My thoughts are simple and focused on basic principles; my message, like that of Jesus, is so straightforward any child can understand it. This is where the power of God shines.

Since my out-of-the-body experience, I have gained a new sensitivity to the Holy Spirit and a greater openness to the supernatural. I feel the spirit of an audience in a way I never could before. As I sense the needs of people, tender compassion for them wells up within me.

I ministered at Melodyland one Sunday evening recently, and one of those who received his healing that night commented, "It wasn't so much what Marvin said, but how he said it." This is one of the key changes I have experienced.

I also have received unshakable faith. Knowing God preserved me through death, I am now able to trust Him for anything. And I no longer fear death, for I have gone beyond and know what awaits me on the other side.

The ability to know things about people that are not revealed except by the Holy Spirit is a supernatural manifestation available to any Christian who asks for it in faith.[3] But there is something about returning from the beyond that makes a person more receptive.

Often a Christian returning from an in-depth out-of-the-body experience will have a global concern. From the perspective of Heaven, the Earth seems a small and lonely place. Its people are one, and all of them need to be won for Christ. In the past I was more concerned about my failures as a minister; global concern was not my focus. Today, I am not entertained by my success, though I'm certainly thankful for it. But down in my heart there is a burning desire to tell everybody about Jesus and what He has in store for them now and in the beyond!

People become more meaningful to those who have been on the other side. During a recent service at Melodyland, Betty Malz of Houston, Texas, told how she had to die to learn how to live. After eleven days of intense suffering, doctors finally decided to operate. She was rushed to a hospital emergency room in Houston with what later was discovered to be a festering, ruptured appendix. A mass of gangrene the size of a man's head had grown steadily over the eleven-day period, covering the pelvic area of her body. Betty was not expected to live.

After forty-four days in a coma, with complications of pneumonia, two bowel blocks, insufficient B-negative blood for needed transfusions and fever of 105 degrees, she was pronounced dead.

Betty visited Heaven, saw the same beautiful city I did, and met with Jesus. Then, through the prayers of a man she never liked—an ugly, crude, uneducated man who stood next to her comatose body one day—she was given the key to her healing and return.

Betty relates what happened as she met with Jesus:

> As I stood there and His light began to stream through my body and heal me, He overhauled my mind and my thinking. It dawned on me all of a sudden that I had been scrambling for popularity, chasing rainbows.
>
> I realized that the only thing on Earth that mattered was people, and yet I had never really liked people.

I told the Lord that if I had one more chance to come back, I would invest my time in people. I believe that is why He allowed me to come back.

I had a love for people when I returned, and my prejudice was gone. My narrow scope of vision regarding church affiliations disappeared, and I realized that we all belong to the majesty of Heaven and God. . . .[4]

A person doesn't have to leave his body to develop this kind of outlook on life. It is a work of the Holy Spirit available to any Christian who will totally surrender his life to Jesus.[5] We need not await the shock of death to jolt us into getting our priorities straight. As we take on the nature of Christ, we can all have a changed attitude.

What about those who claim to have had out-of-the-body experiences but return with no change in their lives? No one can truly meet Jesus and come away unaffected; that did not happen when He was on Earth, and it certainly will not happen now.

Eternal Perspective

Our lives are a continuous thread running from birth to eternity. Because we usually associate life on Earth with a physical body, we tend to consider spirit, soul and body inseparable. Yet, life is so much more than the earthly shell in which the spirit is temporarily imprisoned; it is the very breath of God.[6] Therefore, we need a new perspective that transcends these few years of residence on Earth.

Dying and coming back gave that to me.

Since death is inevitable—unless the Lord returns

first—we must come to understand in our deepest being that dying is merely a passage into another world. From our limited perspective, death seems like the sudden slamming of a door when in reality it is the threshold of immortality.

To what destiny that door opens is up to us. There is no second chance when death is final. Our fate is determined by our relationship to Christ. Is He our Lord and Savior? Have we accepted His gift of salvation and been reborn by His Spirit? Or have we decided to reject Christ and follow other paths to the world beyond?

God will honor our decision on the other side: we can either face His judgment alone, on the worthless chaff of our merits, or we can meet Him prepared by the life-changing power of Jesus Christ, having been declared forgiven of sin, and blameless as we stand before His eternal throne.[7]

From this perspective, we can see that eternal life or eternal death has already begun in our lives. We are endless beings *now*. When death comes, we will exist somewhere on the other side. The question that must be settled is *where*. Christ has declared the alternatives; the decision is ours.

Bridge to Eternity

On my journey into afterlife, I witnessed the splendors awaiting those who trust in God. From this vantage point, I see the urgency of making sure the dying are ready to meet Christ. Even for the person who lies in a coma.

"Never be afraid to go into a hospital room and take hold of the hand of a person and lead them to Christ through the Word of God," Betty Malz says. "You may be the bridge from this life to eternity. While I lay in a coma in the hospital one day, I heard footsteps coming into my room. Soon I heard pages of a Bible being turned, and I heard the voice of a man whom I never liked. He was an ugly person, crude and uneducated, and I was ashamed of him.

"My first impulse was, 'I can't stand this man when I am well. I know I can't take him now. Doesn't he know I'm sick?' But he stood at the foot of my bed and began to read from Psalm 107:20, 'He sent his word, and healed them. . . .' This ugly man suddenly became a beautiful instrument playing sweet music to my dying soul. He was not wise, but God chose to speak through him."

During her testimony at Melodyland, Betty told how this person became the key to her return:

I had a desire to come back to my husband, my 6-year-old and to people and tell them where I had been and of the joy that is there.

As we started back down the hill [located in the realm she visited] I saw the hospital room. . . . I saw Betty but it was as though I heard the Lord say, "God and the Holy Spirit and Jesus have killed the old Betty; we are bringing back a new one."

When I walked down the hill, it was morning . . . sunrise, and the rays of the sun were pouring into my hospital room. Feeling the warmth of the sunbeam as it focused on a spot to the right of my bed, I watched as ivory letters about two inches high rolled down the center of the beam like the tape of a stock market report.

They were John 11:25, "I am the resurrection, and the life: he that believeth in me, though he were dead, yet shall he live."

Betty says she reached up to touch the letters and as she did, pushed the sheet off her face. She continues:

> When I touched them, warmth and strength and life went into my fingers down through my arms and into my body, and I sat up!
> It was the Word of God that became alive to me. He sent His Word and healed me, just as that man I didn't like had read in the Bible.

With death the threshold to the hereafter, it is little wonder Satan awaits just on the other side to deceive those destined to return. For in the process, they become unwitting emissaries of false hope. We cannot, therefore, let one opportunity slide without warning those on the brink of eternity what lies ahead. It is this passion that burns day and night in my soul; it is this vision that lifts my eyes to the horizon of global concern.

Was it worth leaving the glories of the afterlife to return? A thousand times yes! For when I again journey beyond, I will be accompanied by thousands who would never have known those awaiting splendors.

Imagine being transported at an incredible speed through interstellar space toward a world bathed in dazzling hues of rainbow light. Your first glimpse is its brilliance in the far distance, then the glistening golden rays of a walled city. The closer you come, the more its glory shines.

You see next those massive walls built on twelve foundations, garnished with gems each seemingly trying to outdo the other in beauty.

Suddenly in front of you is a gate of solid pearl, one of twelve giving entrance into the city. Through it you see golden streets, transparent as glass. An angel guarding the gate[8] invites you in, where you see splendors of increasing glory ascending to God's throne.

Yet, none of these splendors compares to the real glory of Heaven—Jesus Christ, the King of Kings and the Lord of Lords.

Imagine what it will be like to see Him; to look into His eyes, those deep wells of living love, to put our fingers into jagged holes left by the nails that secured Him to the cross for our sins, to see the crown of pure light that replaced the crown of thorns; to hear His voice as it fills the soul with inexpressible delight; to look upon His face, strong, ageless, expressing eternity, and to see a smile play upon His lips as He welcomes us into His infinite realm.

Yes, every resplendent glory we can envision is there in the city of God.

Now, picture waking up someday—perhaps soon—and discovering that you had not imagined it at all, but had indeed journeyed *on the other side*.

Source Notes

Chapter 1

1 Rev. 21:2.
2 Acts 7:55-58.
3 Ezekiel 10 to 11:1.
4 Dan. 7:9-10.
5 Fox, Lorne F., *Visions of Heaven, Hell and the Cross* (Privately published, P.O. Box 34, Naselle, Wash., n.d.), pp. 25-6.
6 Hagin, Kenneth, *I Believe in Visions* (Fleming H. Revell Company, Old Tappan, N.J., 1972), pp. 48, 50.
7 John 20:25-28.
8 Lindsay, Gordon, ed., *Scenes Beyond the Grave* (Christ for the Nations, Dallas, Tex., 13th ed., 1973), pp. 52-4.

Chapter 2

1 *Déjà vu* is a common experience also known as paramnesia, the illusion of remembering scenes and events when experienced for the first time.
2 Martin, E.G., "Search to Prove the Human Soul Exists," *National Enquirer*, June 30, 1974.
3 Wheeler, David R., *Journey to the Other Side* (ACE Books, 1120 Avenue of the Americas, New York, N.Y. 10036, 1977), p. 84.
4 Martin, *op. cit.*
5 Wheeler, *op. cit.*, p. 74.
6 Ostrander, Sheila, and Schroeder, Lynn, *Psychic Discoveries Behind the Iron Curtain* (Bantam Books, 666 Fifth Avenue, New York, N.Y. 10019, 1970), p 201.
7 1 Thess. 5:23.
8 Heb. 4:12.
9 Gen. 3:19.
10 James 2:26, ". . . The body without the spirit is dead. . . ."
11 Moody, Dr. Raymond Jr., *Life After Life* (Mockingbird Books Inc., P.O. Box 110, Covington, Ga. 30209, 1975), pp. 36-8.
12 *Ibid.*, p. 85.
13 Monroe, Robert A., *Journeys Out of the Body* (Doubleday,

Garden City, N.Y., Anchor Press Ed., 1973), p. 167.

14 *Ibid.*, p. 170.

15 Scott, Rev. Elwood, *Paradise, the City and Throne* (Publisher unknown, printed in 1909), p. 33.

16 Baker, H.A., *Heaven and the Angels* (The Baker Book Concern, 3940 S. 24th Avenue, Minneapolis, Minn., printed in Taiwan, 3rd ed., n.d.), pp. 96, 97.

17 *Ibid.*, pp. 104-5.

18 Matt. 22:30.

19 Gal. 3:26-28.

20 1 Cor. 13:12.

21 Lindsay, *op. cit.*, p. 26.

22 Springer, Rebecca, *Within the Gates* (Formerly *Intra Muros*), edited by Gordon Lindsay (Christ for the Nations, Dallas, Tex., 1971), pp. 9-10.

23 Matt. 17:1-13.

24 Luke 16:19-31. Many leading Bible scholars consider this a literal story, not a parable.

25 Rev. 6:9-11.

26 Ps. 16:10; Luke 23:43; Eph. 4:7-11; 1 Pet. 3:19. For an in-depth study of this concept, see *God's Plan for Man* by Finis Jennings Dake, Dake Bible Sales Inc., P.O. Box 173, Lawrenceville, Ga., 1949, pp. 49-65.

27 Lindsay, *op. cit.*, pp. 61-2.

28 *Ibid.*, pp. 63-6, 68.

Chapter 3

1 "I Looked Down and Saw My 7-Year-Old Son Crying," *National Enquirer*, Feb. 24, 1974.

2 "I Felt Free from All Suffering," *National Enquirer*, Aug. 18, 1974.

3 "I Was Given a Glimpse of Heaven. . .," *National Enquirer*, March 17, 1974.

4 "My Spirit Floated from My Body," *National Enquirer*, June 16, 1974.

5 Moody, *op. cit.*, pp. 23-4.

6 Wheeler, *op. cit.*, p. 137.

7 "I Know I Died," *National Enquirer*, May 5, 1974.

8 "I Floated Out of My Hospital Room," *National Enquirer*, March 17, 1974.

9 "How Two Tiny Trees Proved I'd Had an Out-of-Body Experience," *National Enquirer*, Oct. 17, 1974.

10 Delacour, Jean-Baptiste, *Glimpses of the Beyond*, trans. by

SOURCE NOTES

E.B. Garside (Delacorte Press, New York, N.Y., 1974), p. 31.

11 "I Took a Journey Beyond the Grave," *National Enquirer*, Nov. 12, 1974.

12 Delacour, *op. cit.*, p. 32.

13 "I Felt So Peaceful," *National Enquirer*, May 10, 1977.

14 "I Died at 10:52 A.M." *Reader's Digest*, October 1974, p. 181.

15 Quoted in Wheeler, *op. cit.*, p. 141.

16 Weldon, John, and Levitt, Zola, *Is There Life After Death?* (Harvest House, Irvine, Ca., 1977), p. 46.

17 Osis, Karlis, and Haraldsson, Erlendur, *At the Hour of Death* (Avon Books, New York, N.Y., 1977), pp. 62-3.

18 "I Saw My Long-Dead Mother," *National Enquirer*, Sept. 1, 1974.

19 Delacour, *op. cit.*, p. 6.

20 Wheeler, *op. cit.*, p. 95.

21 "All People Who 'Died,'" *National Enquirer*, May 17, 1977.

22 "Filled With Horror," *National Enquirer*, July 21, 1974.

23 Crookall, Robert, *Out-of-the-Body Experiences, A Fourth Analysis* (University Books Inc., New Hyde Park, N.Y., 1970), pp. 146-9.

24 Monroe, *op. cit.*, p. 175.

25 Yram, *Practical Astral Projection* (Samuel Weiser, New York, N.Y. 1967), p. 75.

26 Moody, *op. cit.*, p. 175.

27 Moody, *Life After Life* (The Reader's Digest Book Section, January 1977), p. 207.

Chapter 4

1 Sherman, Harold, *Your Mysterious Powers of ESP* (a Signet Book from The New American Library Inc., 1301 Avenue of the Americas, New York, N.Y. 10019, 1969), p. 183.

2 *Ibid.*, pp. 180-1.

3 Smith, Susy, *The Enigma of Out-of-Body Travel* (a Signet Book from The New American Library Inc., 1301 Avenue of the Americas, New York, N.Y. 10019, 1965), pp. 13-15.

4 Wheeler, *op. cit.*, pp. 49-51.

5 Greenhouse, Herbert B., *The Astral Journey* (Avon Books, The Hearst Corporation, 959 Eighth Ave., New York, N.Y. 10019, 1974), p. 17.

6 *Ibid.*, p. 10.

7 Ophiel, *The Art and Practice of Astral Projection* (Samuel Weiser, 734 Broadway, New York, N.Y. 10003, 1961), pp. 23-4.

SOURCE NOTES

8 Crookall, *op. cit.*, p. 13.
9 Greenhouse, *op. cit.*, pp. 10, 11.
10 Yram, *op. cit.*, p. 62.
11 Greenhouse, *op. cit.*, pp. 16-19.
12 Yram, *op. cit.*, pp. 52, 110-11.
13 Ophiel, *op. cit.*, p. 24.
14 Sherman, *op. cit.*, p. 183.
15 *Ibid.*, p. 180.
16 *Ibid.*, p. 198.
17 *Ibid.*, pp. 194-5.
18 Monroe, *op. cit.*, p. 127.
19 *Ibid.*, pp. 52, 53.
20 Monroe, *op. cit.*, pp. 120-1.
21 *Ibid.*, pp. 138-9.
22 Greenhouse, *op. cit.*, p. 17.
23 Crookall, *op. cit.*, pp. 24-5.
24 Wheeler, *op. cit.*, pp. 84-5.
25 Smith, *op. cit.*, p. 35.
26 Brod, Michael, based on an interview.
27 Acts 8:39-40.

Chapter 5

1 Johnson, George, and Tanner, Don, *The Bible and the Bermuda Triangle* (Logos International, Plainfield, N.J. 07061, 1976), pp. 20-1.
2 Weldon, John, *UFOs: What on Earth Is Happening?* (Harvest House Publishers, Irvine, Ca., 1975), pp. 120-1.
3 Johnson and Tanner, *op. cit.*, pp. 24-5.
4 Jeffrey, Adi-Kent Thomas, *The Bermuda Triangle* (Warner Paperback Library, P.O. Box 690, New York, N.Y. 10019, 1975), p. 174.
5 Johnson and Tanner, *op. cit.*, pp. 26-7.
6 Possibly a crew member of Flight 19, the five Navy TBM Avengers that disappeared during a routine training mission from Fort Lauderdale Naval Air Station. The object of an intensive ground-sea rescue operation, no trace of the flight was ever located.
7 *National Tattler*, Jan. 26, 1975.
8 Johnson and Tanner, *op. cit.*, pp. 85-115.
9 Phil. 2:9-10.
10 Bergier, Jacques, *Secret Doors of the Earth* (Henry Regnery Co., 180 N. Michigan Ave., Chicago, Ill., 1975), pp. 22-3.

11 2 Cor. 4:4.

12 Monroe, *op. cit.*, p. 74.

13 *Ibid.*, pp. 74-5. A similar observation was reported by
    Marietta Davis when she visited the nether world abode of
    departed spirits. See chapter 2.

14 *Ibid.*, p. 76.

15 *Ibid.*, p. 75.

16 "I Heard My Father's Spirit Calling Me," *National
    Enquirer*, April 7, 1974.

17 "I Floated Up to the Gates of Heaven," *National Enquirer*,
    June 10, 1975.

18 "I Took a Journey to the Depths of Hell and the Gates of
    Heaven and Was Rejected by Both," *National Enquirer*,
    Dec. 10, 1974.

19 Delacour, *op. cit.*, pp. 12-13.

20 *Ibid.*, p. 113.

21 Moody, *op. cit.*, pp. 45-6.

22 John 8:12.

23 1 John 1:5.

24 Matt. 28:2-4; John 20:12; Luke 24:1-4; Rev. 10:1.

25 2 Cor. 11:14.

26 Ezekiel 28.

27 Luke 2:9-15.

28 Moody, *op. cit.*, pp. 107-8.

29 Taken from her testimony given at Massapequa Tabernacle,
    Long Island's Revival Center, 4100 Jerusalem Ave.,
    Massapequa, N.Y. 11758, where she and her husband were
    delivered from the occult by power of God.

30 Merlin, Barbara, "One of the Comedian's Closest Friends
    Reveals Jack Benny's Amazing Psychic Experience on His
    Death Bed," *National Enquirer*, Aug. 31, 1976, p. 41.

31 "I Saw My Dead Father Across a River," *National
    Enquirer*, March 24, 1974.

32 Rev. 22:5.

33 Moody, *op. cit.*, pp. 70, 90.

34 Wheeler, *op. cit.*, pp. 43-4.

35 Adapted from his testimony printed in a privately published
    leaflet.

36 Delacour, *op. cit.*, pp. 22-5.

37 Monroe, *op. cit.*, p. 94.

38 *Ibid.*, pp. 95-7.

39 Space is considered the third dimension in that it contains the
    three dimensions of length, breadth and height. Time is
    viewed as the fourth dimension. The fifth is the realm of the

spirit. No one knows how many dimensions exist, but the possibilities are infinite.

40 Monroe, *op. cit.*, p. 117.
41 Eph. 2:2, 6:12.

Chapter 6

1 Wilkerson, Ralph, *Beyond and Back* (Melodyland Publishers, 10 Freedman Way, Anaheim, Ca., 1977), pp. 95-6.
2 *Ibid.*, pp. 97-8, 102-4.
3 John 14:6, "Jesus saith. . . I am the way, the truth, and the life. . . ." John 8:12, "Then spake Jesus again . . . I am the light of the world: he that followeth me shall not walk in darkness. . . ."
4 "I Saw Heaven's Beautiful Mansions," *National Enquirer*, Sept. 8, 1974.
5 Wilkerson, *op. cit.*, pp. 106-8.
6 Exodus 34:29-35.
7 Baker, H.A., *The Three Worlds* (The Osterhus Publishing House, 4500 W. Brendwoy, Minneapolis, Minn., n.d., printed in Taiwan), pp. 284-9.
8 "I Know I Died and Went on a Strange Journey into the Unknown," *National Enquirer*, May 5, 1974.
9 Monroe, *op. cit.*, p. 262.
10 "I Spoke to Jesus and He Gave Me the Chance to Live My Life for Him," *National Enquirer*, June 9, 1974.
11 Baker, *op. cit.*, pp. 289-93.

Chapter 7

1 Luke 11:13; Acts 2:1-4.
2 Acts 2:6; 1 Cor. 14:13-14.
3 2 Kings 2:9-14.

Chapter 8

1 Acts 21:10-11.
2 Heb. 1:1-2.
3 1 Cor. 13:10.
4 Eph. 4:11.
5 1 Cor. 14:3.
6 Deut. 18:10-11; Rev. 22:15.
7 1 Cor. 14:31.

227

SOURCE NOTES

8 Published by the Kenneth Hagin Evangelistic Association, P.O. Box 50126, Tulsa, Okla. 74150.
9 1 Cor. 12:8-10.
10 Isa. 28:21.
11 Isa. 42:13.
12 Rev. 3:8.
13 1 Cor. 16:9.
14 Matt. 6:4.
15 Ps. 133:2.
16 Isa. 45:2-3.
17 Isa. 55:12.
18 Wilkerson, *op. cit.*, pp. 16-18.
19 1 Cor. 14:29; 1 John 4:1.
20 Wilkerson, *op. cit.*, pp. 19-20.

Chapter 9

1 Rev. 21:10-27; 22:1-5; 1 Cor. 2:9.
2 Rev. 7:9.
3 Rev. 21:15-17.
4 Rev. 2:7; Luke 23:43.
5 Baker, H.A., *Visions Beyond the Veil* (Whitaker Books, 504 Laurel Drive, Monroeville, Pa. 15146, 1973), pp. 5-8, 49-61, 70, 71.
6 2 Cor. 12:2-4.
7 Baker, H.A., *Heaven and the Angels* (The Baker Book Concern, 3940 S. 24th Ave., Minneapolis, Minn. 55406, printed in Taiwan, 3rd ed., not copyrighted), pp. 54-9.
8 Springer, *op. cit.*, pp. 27-8. Note: "cherubs" are not baby angels as they are so often pictured on valentines. Cherubim (plural form of cherub) are types of celestial beings lower in rank than seraphim, another angelic order. Seraphim have three sets of wings, according to Isa. 6:2.
9 Baker, *Heaven and the Angels*, p. 63.
10 Scott, *op. cit.*, p. 14.
11 Lindsay, *op. cit.*, p. 26.
12 Springer, *op. cit.*, p. 18.
13 Rev. 1:13-15.
14 Fox, *op. cit.*, p. 29.

Chapter 10

1 Isa. 14:13.
2 Job 26:7.

3 Ps. 48:1-2.
4 Prov. 13:22.
5 Gen. 1:26.
6 Gen. 1:28.
7 John 10:10, 11:25.
8 Matt. 28:20.

Chapter 11

1 2 Cor. 12:2-4.
2 1 Cor. 13:9-12; Deut. 18:10-11.
3 1 Cor. 12:4-11; John 16:13.
4 Olson, Bruce, *For This Cross I'll Kill You* (Creation House Inc., 499 Gundersen Dr., Carol Stream, Ill. 60187, 1973).
5 Acts 2:4-6.
6 Rom. 11:25-27.
7 Matt. 28:4; John 18:6; Acts 9:4.

Chapter 12

1 Gen. 15:1-6.
2 Deut. 34:1-3.
3 Ezek. 11:1, 37:1.
4 Acts 10:10-16.
5 Acts 16:9.
6 Acts 7:55-56.
7 Rev. 1:10, 4:1.
8 Joel 2:28; Acts 2:17.
9 John 16:13.
10 Mark 16:17-18; John 14:12-13.
11 Matt. 24:14; Col. 1:6; Acts 1:8, 2:17-21.
12 Wilkerson, *op. cit.*, pp. 131-2.
13 1 Cor. 12:4-11.
14 2 Sam. 12:1-15.
15 Acts 5:1-11.
16 Luke 5:3-7.
17 John 4:16-18.
18 Luke 22:7-13.
19 Lev. 20:27; 1 Sam. 15:23; Isa. 8:19; Micah 5:12.
20 From an interview with Mary-Ann Brod, August 3, 1977.
21 Joel 2:28-29.
22 Matt. 24:14.

SOURCE NOTES

Chapter 13

1 There were two compartments of light in the tabernacle of the Old Testament: the holy place with the lampstand and the holy of holies with the Shekinah, or manifested glory of God. What I saw in my hospital room was this Shekinah glory in the person of God's Son, Jesus Christ. Note Exodus 27:20, Scofield notes; Exodus 25:31; 2 Cor. 4:6; Exodus 40:34-8.

2 Wilkerson, *op. cit.*, pp. 60-1.

3 John 16:13; 1 Cor. 12:31.

4 From her testimony given during the 1977 charismatic clinic, Melodyland Christian Center, Anaheim, Calif.

5 Gal. 5:22-4.

6 Gen. 2:7; Job 33:4.

7 Rom. 3:23-6; Eph. 5:27.

8 Rev. 21:12.

If you enjoyed this book may we recommend other best sellers available where paperbacks are sold or use this order form:

Qty.		Price	Total
____	Daughter of Destiny—Kuhlman—Buckingham	$1.95	_____
____	Day the Dollar Dies—Cantelon	1.45	_____
____	Eldridge Cleaver: Reborn—Oliver	1.95	_____
____	Healed of Cancer—Jo Lawson	1.95	_____
____	Hustler for the Lord—Larry Jones	1.95	_____
____	The Jesus Factor—David Manuel	1.95	_____
____	Move That Mountain—Jim Bakker	1.95	_____
____	On the Other Side—Ford, Balsiger, Tanner	1.95	_____
____	Prison to Praise—Merlin Carothers	1.50	_____
____	Run Baby Run—Nicky Cruz	1.50	_____
____	Shout It From the Housetops—Pat Robertson	1.95	_____
____	The Big 3 Mountain-Movers—Jim Bakker	1.95	_____
____	Visions of Jesus—Chet & Lucile Huyssen	1.95	_____
		Add 10% *for Shipping*	_____
		Total	_____

☐ Send Free Order Form—over 250 titles
☐ Send Free Information about *Logos Journal* Magazine
   Include payment to:
    LIF BOOKS
    Box 191
    Plainfield, NJ 07061

Name _____

Address _____

City _____State_____

                   Zip_____

If you have visited the other side, have any comments about the subject, or want Marvin Ford to address your group or organization, he would like to hear from you.

Address correspondence to:

Marvin Ford
P.O. Box 1667
Whittier, Calif. 90609
